Mind Manipulation and Persuasion

Learn the secrets of mental control to analyze, influence, and manipulate people through body language and understand what they are saying using emotional intelligence, psychology, and empathy.

BY

Chris Cooper

by the trademark owner. All trademarks and brands within this book are for clarifying purposes only and are the owned by the owners themselves, not affiliated with this document.

Table of contents

Mind Manipulation - Part 1

INTRODUCTION — 7

CHAPTER 1: FUNDAMENTALS OF MIND MANIPULATION — 10

1.1 BASIC IDEAS — 10
1.2 THE MANIPULATIVE BEHAVIOR — 11
1.3 CONCEPT OF INFLUENCE AND PERSUASION — 13
1.4 MIND MANIPULATION AND BRAINWASHING — 16
1.5 TYPES OF MIND MANIPULATION — 17
1.6 WHY DO PEOPLE MANIPULATE OTHERS — 19

CHAPTER 2: MIND MANIPULATION TECHNIQUES — 22

2.1 WAYS OF MIND MANIPULATION — 22
2.2 MANIPULATION STRATEGIES — 26
2.3 EMOTIONAL MANIPULATION TECHNIQUES — 32
2.4 TECHNIQUES OF PSYCHOLOGICAL MANIPULATION — 37
2.5 HOW TO MANIPULATE OTHERS USING DARK PSYCHOLOGY — 38
2.6 DEFINING DESIRED OUTCOMES — 42

CHAPTER 3: MIND MANIPULATION FACTS AND FICTION — 36

3.1 THE REALITY OF MIND CONTROL — 36
3.2 THE REALISTIC SCOPE OF MIND CONTROL — 37
3.3 MYTHS ABOUT MIND CONTROL — 38

CHAPTER 4: MIND MANIPULATION IN EVERYDAY LIFE — 52

4.1 HOW TO SPOT A MANIPULATOR — 52
4.2 VICTIMS OF MANIPULATION — 67
4.3 POSSIBILITY OF COUNTERATTACK — 76
4.4 SIX MAXIMS FOR MANIPULATION HANDLING — 81
4.5 FACTORS AFFECTING THE EFFECTIVENESS — 82
4.6 A GROWING PROBLEM — 83

CHAPTER 5: NLP — 84

5.1 WHAT IS NLP — 84
5.2 HOW OTHERS ARE USING NLP ON YOU — 85
5.3 PRACTICAL STEPS TO ATTAIN THESE SKILLS — 88
5.3 USING NLP FOR EFFECTIVE LEADERSHIP — 89

5.4 MIND MANAGEMENT FOR LOVE AND RELATIONSHIP WITH NLP — 91

CHAPTER 6: HOW TO COPE WITH MANIPULATIONS — 92

6.1 HOW TO COPE WITH MANIPULATIONS IN LOVE LIFE — 92
6.2 HOW TO DEAL WITH SOCIAL LIFE MANIPULATIONS — 95
6.3 HOW TO TREAT BUSINESS MANIPULATIONS — 98
6.4 HOW TO DEAL WITH MANIPULATIVE EMPATHY — 100
6.5 HOW TO DEAL WITH THE MANIPULATIVE CON — 101

CONCLUSION — 103

The Psychology of Persuasion - Part 2

INTRODUCTION — **105**

CHAPTER 1: WHAT IS PERSUASION AND INFLUENCE? — 105

1.1 A SHORT HISTORY OF PERSUASION: — 110
1.2 WHAT IS PERSUASION IN THE MODERN AGE? — 119
1.3 THE POWER OF INFLUENCE — 121
1.4 CONGRUENT ATTITUDES — 125
1.5 CONTROL BODY LANGUAGE AND VOICE TONE — 126
1.6 BEHAVIORAL CONSISTENCY — 131

CHAPTER 2: LAWS OF PERSUASION — 134

2.1 LAWS OF PERSUASION — 134
2.2 SECRETS METHODS OF PERSUASION — 143

CHAPTER 3: DARK PSYCHOLOGY, PERSUASION AND MIND MANIPULATION — 153

3.1 WHAT IS DARK PSYCHOLOGY? — 162
3.2 MIND CONTROL TECHNIQUES — 162
3.4 HOW TO CREATE A CONNECTION — 167
3.5 CREATE AN EXPECTATION — 170
3.6 STEER THE PERSON TO YOUR POINT OF VIEW — 175

CHAPTER 4: DEALING AGAINST PERSUASION — 178

4.1 HOW TO DEAL AGAINST PERSUASION — 178
4.2 UNMASKING DARK PERSUADER — 182

4.3 TIPS TO DEAL AGAINST PERSUASION 186

4.5 HOW MANIPULATIVE BEHAVIOR DEVELOPS? 186

4.6 The difference between persuasion and manipulation. ... 190

4.7 ART OF PERSUASION IN BUSINESS 191

CONCLUSION 198

REFERENCES 202

Mind Manipulation - Part 1

Introduction

Manipulation is everywhere, but you can't always see it. Because of this, you may compare it to many different everyday habits we are not still aware of. Manipulators act as spiders or vindictive insects, still lurking around, which we don't know. You don't even feel it when they bite, but surely you will notice the wound long after the initial attack.

To live happily in our world, we need to start becoming more conscious of exploitation. Recognizing that someone is trying to control, you will make it much easier to stay out of their controlled grasp. The book will take you back to a place of personal independence, where you will be able to make your own decisions regularly.

If you begin to identify manipulation better, how it develops, and how it has affected your life, then navigation without it will only become more comfortable. Interacting with others can include doing your best to prevent it from happening healthily. Stopping ourselves from being manipulated, though, is not the only important thing we will be talking about.

We'll be paying close attention to how you can make yourself a convincing person. Even though you may have been hurt by manipulation in the past, or also damage your mental health by being the manipulator yourself, there is hope, now that we can work for ourselves towards a better future. This is done by becoming a person who is inspiring and potentially influential.

Manipulation is harmful, but it can become a beneficial force when viewed in a more positive light. If you can be a convincing person, and not only get what you want but also satisfy other people's needs, then it will be easier for you to get the things you want most in life.

Rather than always doing things you don't enjoy, is the "yes man" or allowing people to take advantage of your good nature, you can become just as influential as the people who have previously tried to control you.

You may even be at a stage where you hate coercion entirely. Why would you like to do something for others that, in the past, has caused you to grieve? This sort of thinking is because we were only aware of the harmful, manipulative types. To lead a harmonious life, we must become convincing people who know what we want. Not only that but ensuring we have the tools to understand how to get those things.

In this process, the first important step is to investigate the types of the personality of manipulators, as well as the people they commonly follow. You may have heard of the standard kind of personality, "Narcissist," a person who only cares about himself and gets the things he wants. Narcissists might benefit from empathy or highly sensitive people who are more concerned with other people's wellbeing.

After that, we will further discuss constructive manipulative attitudes and how, in your relationships, you can incorporate some of those beneficial behaviors. If you can do that, you'll be better able to see how positive influence will change your life for the better.

Besides that, we'll also be learning how our bodies interact, the signs and answers we're giving out, and what other people might take away from our body language. Apart from our verbal communication, the more you will understand power, the easier it will be to stop being affected by yourself and to persuade those around you better.

After we understand what all of this means, the rest of the influential tips we'll share throughout the book will be more comfortable to learn and practice. Note that you should be affecting others only positively. Though it may seem more straightforward to manipulate negatively those you want something from, the person you'd most hurt in this process will be yourself. Look for ways to influence each other positively, so that you can benefit both parties.

Chapter 1: Fundamentals of Mind Manipulation

For the purposes of this book, a clear definition of manipulation is of the most significant importance. Instances of manipulation and several other forms of influence will be complicated to separate without understanding precisely what manipulation is about.

While you probably have your own idea of what constitutes coercion, it is necessary to follow the book concept to make meaningful, practical advice in later chapters.

1.1 Basic Ideas

In the broadest sense, manipulation is an attempt to influence others ' actions or perceptions. Some meanings include' the use of coercive, misleading or otherwise exploitative methods' or similar to differentiate between coercion and other activities affecting such as persuasion.

This poses even more issues such as "exploitative" stuff. It is quite easy to describe frustration as a deliberate deception or modification of the facts. Yet trickery actually stops persuasion? Presumably, you will not mention the times that you came late to work because of hangovers, in a job interview; is this manipulation? It may be argued that anyone recruiting a job also understands that people are likely to stress their positive characteristics and draw attention from the negative aspects. It is not automatically unethical to withhold such details in this case. Intention can, therefore, also play a part in deciding the ethics of violence and distinguishing between exploitation and other types of power.

For now, putting ethics aside, in that broad definition, there is another term worthy of attention. The concept of manipulation as "efforts" suggests that, regardless of success or failure, manipulation continues to be exploited. Ironically, those who have little success in influencing others than those who excel are more likely to gain a manipulative reputation.

You may be able to point to a manipulative person in your circle, perhaps a relative or colleague. Thought, though, of how others perceive them. Were they identified as a manipulator? Does this impact their success? The reaction can also be complicated. If someone at work by their peers is considered deceptive and still controls the boss, they may still be regarded as good. Specific goals are important when it comes to influencing others. It allows you to make fair, unbiased decisions that are important to success.

At this point, we have so many questions and very few answers to them. The remaining chapter ties some loose ends and provides a summary that will make a difference to the rest of the book.

1.2 The Manipulative Behavior

If you ever felt like something is off in close relationships or casual meetings, you are under pressure, under stress, or even feel as if you have more questions than normal–it could be manipulation.

"Manipulation is the socially destructive psychological strategy employed by people who cannot know what they want and what they need," says Sharie Stine's, a California-based violence and toxicity therapist. "There are many different forms of coercion, from a pushy salesperson to an emotionally abusive partner — and certain conducts are easier to detect than others." Those who try to manipulate others try to control others.

Experts clarify the telltale signs here that you could be the victim of exploitation.

- **Factors**

Stine's notes that coercive conduct includes three factors:
- Anxiety
- Obligation
- Guilt

"If coerced by someone, you're mentally compelled to do something; you actually don't really want to do something," she says. You may feel frightened, obligated, or guilty to do so.

She points to two usual manipulators: "the bully" and "the victims." She claims that a bully makes you feel afraid and can manipulate you by violence, threats, or intimidation. The perpetrator instills in her target a sense of remorse. "The victim usually hurts," Stine says. But while manipulators sometimes play the victim, it adds that the reality is that they caused the problem.

Stine's says a person targeted by manipulators who sometimes play the victim tries to help the manipulator from being guilty. Objectives like this also feel responsible for helping the survivor to relieve their suffering by doing whatever they can.

The manipulation is a form of deliberate manipulation, described as an attempt by one person or party (the manipulator), typically with the intention of attaining an objective in the interests of the manipulator, to change the mindset and behavior of another person and party (the target).

There is no bad inference or whether or not the manipulator is working against the goal. All that is possible. This generates frustration that is not limited to abstract ethical principles even if that doesn't mean that you, too, will sacrifice your morals!

- **Examples of manipulation**

Some are normal in daily life, while others are associated with special or dramatic events. There is little theoretical difference between individual and wide-ranging manipulation. Almost always, the same principles apply, but between, say, competing nations the practicalities of manipulation techniques such as frustration can be more complicated. Its examples can be found in:

- Business world
- Marketing
- Public relations
- Military strategy
- professional strategy

1.3 Concept of influence and persuasion

Manipulation, paradigm manipulation, brainwashing, mental control, coercive persuasion, coercive control, malignant use of group dynamics, and many others are also known as mind control. The fact is that there are so many names to indicate the lack of agreement that allows for confusion and exploitation (especially by those who use it secretly for their own benefit!!) Let's accept that mind control comes under the umbrella of persuasion and power-how to alter people's attitudes and behaviors.

Some will say the whole thing is a fraud. And when it says so, important distinctions are ignored. It is much more useful to think about power as a continuum. At one end, we have ethical and respectable influences which value the person and his or her rights. At the other end, we have disruptive forces that rob the person of his or her identity, individuality, and ability to think critically or logically.

A one-on-one cult is an intimate relationship in which one person takes advantage of his or her power to manipulate and abuse the other, such as teacher/student, therapist/client, pastor/worshipper, and wife/husband. This cultic relationship is a modification of the larger groups and maybe even more destructive because one person is centered all the time and attention.

- Manipulation and Influence

The modern world has embraced the term "influence" for people who follow broad social media and who are able to influence others with their messages. It takes no particularly critical mind to recognize the source of this term as advertising. When consumer behavior changes, marketers have taken note of and continually look to harness the power of influencers to gain attention for goods. This is done differently by paid or unpaid sponsorships, promotional deals, and contracts.

In some cases, influencers announce these deals while in others, they do not. Ethical questions are again posed, particularly if an influencer is ostensibly only a happy customer but, in secret, on the payroll of the company which sells the product.

The entire moral dilemma could definitely have been prevented if advertisers instead used the word manipulator! Okay, it's hardly surprising that they didn't. What this highlights is that while people expect advertisers to be deceptive, it is still impossible to confess to it. Instagram stars are happily listing themselves on their profile page as influencers with no negative connotations, apparently.

But the intentions of many influencers, particularly those who work with advertisers, are inherently deceptive. It is not even a grey area issue. Influencers tend to sell goods to their followers so that they can make money. It is impossible to know whether the company will help everyone it affects, nor is it possible to know its financial situation or any particular circumstances. In this situation, the influencer prioritizes its own interests.

Manipulation does not mean trying to harm others. However, it needs to put one's own goals and interests first, to some extent. That is only part of the puzzle.

Therefore, it is best and most rational to refer to influence as a parent concept of manipulation; one that involves coercion and other forms of control, such as inspiration and emulation.

- **Manipulation and Persuasion**

These terms may seem diametrically opposed, with persuasion serving as the "honest" form of manipulation in which the actor is at the forefront of his thoughts and opinions. It will be more useful to consider persuasion as a tier below coercion.

Therefore, persuasion becomes a tool of coercion, which is a means of control. One of the strongest motivational mechanisms also happens to be persuasion. How often have you been in discussion with someone else just to hold their hands up and say, "I admit, you're absolutely right?" These occasions can probably be counted on one hand.

It may be easy to persuade someone that smoking is unhealthy, but is it easy to persuade them to quit? If so, politicians would not see the need or benefit from imposing heavy taxes on tobacco products to dissuade consumption. The government is attempting to regulate the intake of tobacco according to the definition of this book and to achieve that end using a variety of methods such as persuasion.

What other causes, then? And other forms of manipulation? Well, deception needs to be deliberate, and it should have some sort of goal–even if that goal is merely to create anarchy. A great director will affect the work of many others, but it obviously varies from exploitation. The filmmaker does not plan to influence others (although they may), rather they gain influence by responding to their work by others, contributing to inspiration and even emulation.

Similarly, persuasion is not the only manipulative method one could employ. Lying is one simple alternative, a type of disappointment. Lying and being credited will inevitably change people's perception of the lie. Whether that is effective or not is still exploitation, as has already been developed.

Unlike power, persuasion is not suffering from quite the same image problem as manipulation. In fact, it is seen as a positive thing to be able to make a "persuasive argument" Although it has a sinister tinge; the phrase "I can be very persuasive" implies some exertion of power over another individual — maybe even an assault. Often, when managers refer to soft skills as "persuasion," it is right to consider this as a deceptive euphemism. At the very least, in part.

1.4 Mind Manipulation and Brainwashing

Steve Hassan distinguishes interestingly between brainwashing and mind control. In brainwashing, he says the victim knows the aggressor is an enemy. Prisoners of war, for example, know that the person doing the brainwashing or torture is an enemy, and they often understand that staying alive depends on changing their belief system. We are forced to do things they normally wouldn't do, often with physical strength. However, when the victim flees from the influence of the enemy, the consequences of brainwashing often go away.

Mind manipulation is more subtle and sophisticated as the manipulator is often considered a relative or mentor so that the victim is not really trying to defend himself. In fact, he or she may be a' willing' participant, and they often willingly provide private information, which is then used against them to continue mind control, believing the manipulator has in mind their best interests.

Which makes mind manipulation as dangerous, if not more so, than physical coercion. That, in other words, can be even more effective than torture, physical abuse, drugs, etc.

That deserves repeating itself. For mind manipulation, there may be no physical force or abuse, but it can actually be much more effective for manipulating a human.

That's because coercion will change behavior, but coercive persuasion (mind manipulation) can change creeds, behaviors, perceptions, and behavioral processes (basically a personality shift). And, the 'victim' willingly and deliberately takes part in the reforms, thinking they are better off!

So then, it's very hard to accept that they've been deceived so manipulated by someone they trusted and loved, and is one of the reasons people don't find it easy to understand mind control. Even if the individual is free from the influence of the deceptive personality, attitudes, values, and actions remain, mainly because the victim thinks they have made those decisions themselves (the consequences of the decisions we make are greater and longer-lasting than the decisions we realize we've been pushed to make), and partly because the person doesn't want to accept it.

1.5 Types of Mind Manipulation

All interpersonal contact uses coercion. Every deception is unnecessary and egoistic.

There are three types of manipulation:

- **Negative or Malicious Manipulation**

What most of us think of when we hear the word "manipulation?"

- *Example*

This manipulation covertly manipulates someone's actions, generally knowingly, to get something that you want at their expense. For instance, to blackmail.

- **Conscious or Unconscious Manipulation**

Conscious or unconscious manipulation is 99 percent of all the manipulations.

- *Example*

According to the social norms of interpersonal communication. Being nice to the cashier at the grocery store. Or that you are good to them. In doing so, we ensure our society has a relationship that could be of benefit down the line. You could choose not to exploit and not to communicate with them.

- **Positive Manipulation**

Usually, this type of manipulation deals with the intentional contact where both parties profit.

- *Example*

A father tells his kid not to play in the driveway.

These three types of coercion are fundamentally egoistic. After all, we are simply greedy creatures. We can't help stop it. There isn't much violence coming with ill-intentioned intent.

1.6 Why do People Manipulate Others

Why do manipulators control others?

Chronicle manipulation is often used as a survival mechanism in a difficult or competitive environment, especially in the absence of relative power and control. Pathological exploitation can also result from personal, social, cultural, or professional conditioning. Take into account the following three possible causes:

- **Fear and indignity**

Fear that this individual will not, as things stand, achieve the desired result from his own merits. This life will not be helpful to him and others. This life is positioned against this person and others.

It is a fear that others will get something they don't and that there are limited resources in a world of a dog eating dogs that must be covered and managed to survive socially, physically, or financially. What will my life be if I don't do that? And if I do not, somebody's going to take the upper hand over me.

Let's dig deeper now. The fear behind coercion is due to a person's lack of integrity.

This means, I don't live for myself worthy of life, and I'm not worthy of life and other people in my best interests with a heart. How a person perceives the relationship between himself and life is primarily whether he sees himself. Therefore, to simplify it, the real belief is: I'm unworthy.

- **Family History**

Has some manipulative family members influenced the person concerned in his or her life? Was the dynamic family battle for economic or social survival? Have there been competition for power, authority, love, and affection, relationships and approval, rank and privilege, monetary and material resources, or other real and perceived "advantage" types? Was there any power struggle between members of families or against "outsiders" for more strength, influence, benefits, and rewards!

- ## The Need to Control the Environment

People who exploit others often do so because they feel that they need to regulate their world and the atmosphere, an instinct that often comes from deep fear or anxiety; it is not healthy behavior. Exploitation can keep the manipulator from relating to its authentic self and can lead to many ill effects. Manipulation can lead to exploitation.

- ## Social weakness

This has the person encountered any social deficiencies or drawbacks during their training years? Did she meet "exclusion" in any way (social, political, cultural, or professional) and wanted to be part of the accepted norm?

- ## Indirect influence and power

It indicates that there have been financial, technical, or cultural norms that promote art, scheme, negotiation, trafficking, abuse of human weakness, the impression of Machiavellian impotence, or other forms of indirect power and influence? Some occupations, for example, are much more likely than others to persuade people. Some societies normalize organizational and social interactions as cooperative agreements, while others do not. Several leaders have announced their intention to convince others to view things from their viewpoint. If one of these powers was applied to an individual, these coercive tactics might have been internalized into compartmental norms.

- **Lack of awareness**

Sometimes, there is a lack of awareness when we don't know that we are responsible for our own reality. Unconsciousness is the inability to directly correlate the events of one's life with the inner level of being. Unconscious people assume that coercion leads to results in a perceived' insecure climate,' given those results that don't provide lasting gratification and end up returning to the square once and again, emotionally or literally. Then there must be another trick to stop the pain of this!
Why doesn't manipulation pay off the quick fix? Since violence is not an appropriate or sincere practice. Trying to balance fear, pain, and unworthiness is a defensive response.
This is a deliberate action not associated with the greater good consciousness. The primary unconsciousness level is the failure to understand that we are all One. Therefore, the personal result is non-authenticity by trying to gain rather than authenticity through coercion.
In conclusion, coercion, often starting with survival or a competitive instinct of self-preservation, becomes narcissistic exploitation and violence, in the worst cases. Self-awareness, honesty, dignity, proactive problem-solving abilities, and positive communication and relationship skills are clear alternatives to manipulative behavior.

Chapter 2: Mind manipulation techniques

This chapter addresses several tools and methods for controlling the mind using emotional and psychological appeal. Some tips are also given on how to employ dark psychology to manipulate others.

2.1 Ways of Mind Manipulation

This topic attempts to look at some of the specific ways in which others' minds are manipulated. The section addresses explicitly hypnosis, manipulation, persuasion, and brainwashing as techniques for mind control.

- **Brainwashing**

As the name suggests, brainwashing involves ways to denounce or forget people's beliefs and replace them with new ones. It's clear from this definition alone that this is a very powerful form of manipulation. Brainwashing, like all other methods of coercion, has both positive and negative aspects. For example, the positive may be due to the need for survival such as when you are relocating to a new environment. Over time, your new acquaintances' way of life will rub off on you as you fight to fit in.

There are, however, two forms of brainwashing that are of interest to us in this section. The first has already been addressed and includes media brainwashing of people. The second is forced and is often done on a personal level as it requires a high level of seclusion to succeed. The former method of brainwashing involves a channel that most people like the radio, or any other type of mass media, can access. The audiences of such media are limited in their choices to execute it successfully so that they have no other media choice. This way, they will listen to or watch any broadcast brainwashing programs. Another feature of related programs is repetitive play. The human mind is much more evil than most people care to think. If something is taught repeatedly over so long, it starts internalizing the teachings, taking them as truths. Truths are contextual, after all.

The second, stronger form of brainwashing, takes advantage of one's emotional vulnerability to plant new ideas and thoughts in someone's mind. The process involves putting one in complete seclusion from the outside, then using different tactics to break down both emotionally. Physical abuse of the subjects is often resorted to in order to achieve the necessary state of emotional breakdown for brainwashing to occur. This includes actions such as the denial of sleep, famine, personal space invasion, beatings, among others. The target will be exposed to such awful conditions as long as it takes to get them to a point where they give up in life. While they are emotionally broken down, they are constantly reminded of being wrong about everything, and of being worthless. The subjects come to believe this sooner or later and find that they have nothing more to live for.

This is when initiating the next stage of brainwashing. Having given up on life, the topic is being offered a way out. The person will naturally cling to anything under the circumstances, and will, therefore, be receptive to anything he is told. While the new ideals are being imparted, the topic will be reinforced positively to show initiative and to apply them. This is a move toward permanence. The isolation is necessary so as not to affect the' molding process' by the external environment or other people.

- **Hypnosis**

Hypnosis is a voluntary association between the hypnotist and the hypnotized, where the former guides the latter by suggestions that are considered deceptive to new realities. Hypnosis has many uses aside from entertainment purposes, which are common to many people. This manipulation is perhaps related to the art of placebo treatment in which patients were observed to cure despite being treated with non-active drugs.

It is not the positive use we are concerned with, as the therapeutic applications of hypnosis. Our concern is when the hypnotizer starts manipulating the target for his or her own benefit. The hypnotist can even manipulate the subject against his will at some stage, and this is where the line has to be drawn. To understand how this can be done, you need to explain exactly how hypnosis works. The hypnotist does not induce a person to the state but rather guides them towards it slowly. This means that if you get hypnotized or not, it's ultimately upon you and not the hypnotist.

How this works is that you will be guided by the hypnotist through suggestions to achieve a changed mental state where you become open to suggestions and control. In this altered state, for example, the hypnotist can recommend you forget you're during pain. When you forget, the pain actually ceases to manifest physically. Given such power over you, it means that something can be suggested by the hypnotist, and you will. At this stage of hypnosis, you are simply the slave of the hypnotist, who is going to do or move as ordered.

Research shows that apart from allowing one to acquire an altered state of mind, hypnosis can also be used to alter people's thoughts on different issues. It is exactly here that hypnotic manipulation sets in. The moment someone else tries to influence your thoughts or perceptions about something, that's considered manipulation. It is even more so when the person being influenced is put in a vulnerable position, which is hypnosis for our case.

- **Persuasion**

Persuasion, as a technique of mind control, may not strike many people. This is because the definition of the term in the textbook means one person is persuading the other to do something. Nevertheless, persuasion can accomplish a significant amount of coercion, as will be shown in this segment. Persuasion can be accomplished in various ways, some of which are:

- Reasoning with your objective
- By charm
- By patience
- By threatening

All human interactions involve a huge amount of persuasion. That mind-control technique is so prevalent that most people are rarely aware of its existence, let alone appreciate its gravity. When you try to buy something from a business person, each of you is trying to convince the other. The businessman might try to convince you that a particular item is a top quality and you might try to get him to lower the price. When you talk to your friend or colleague about politics, you might be trying to persuade him or her to look at things from your perspective. Defense attorneys often try to convince the jurors of the innocence of their clients while the prosecution tries to persuade them to do the same. From these few examples it is clear that persuasion makes a substantial part of our daily lives.

- **Deception**

Deception often acts as a psychological deception. This is where a person tells another person lies with the intention of causing them to alter their beliefs or acts. The person who is being fooled will not have accurate information to go within making any decisions based on the deception. Which means the deceiver has the ability to distort their beliefs or actions as they wish. Deception manifests in a variety of ways just like the other mental-control techniques discussed. The first is through mudslinging and slander covered up under leadership manipulation. This is a type of deception which is used to manipulate the electorate's minds about different candidates for different elective positions.

The second type of deceit is sleight of hand that was covered in the Three Card Monte under manipulation. This was deceit for the primary purpose of robbing the victim. Most of the methods of deception that were addressed in detail and had some degree of fraud in them. This is because you often have to keep your real intentions secret regardless of who you are dealing with, in order to manipulate others effectively. Whether you're dealing with your best friend or spouse doesn't matter; any sort of deception is a fraud, and if uncovered, it is a recipe for chaos.

2.2 Manipulation strategies

We developed four categories to help you organize the techniques of manipulation in a meaningful way. The order is regulated by the manipulator's technique or goal.

The four basic strategies are:

- Blockade Strategy
- Enforcement Strategy

- Sabotage in Conversation
- Sabotage after Conversation
- **The blockade strategy**

The manipulator wants to prevent its interlocutor from reaching its destination with the blockade strategy. He usually wants to keep talking but does not pursue his own goal. A blockade may be defensive or passive, but it may also be offensively or actively tackled. Here are just a few examples of such practices.

Defensive-passive procedures:

Defensive passive procedures include steps as given below:

Insist on your own point of view

- Deny Explanation
- Block Information from your own point of view
- Do not Answer to Questions
- Do not want to Understand
- Dodge
- Hiding behind False Interests

For example, Mrs. Müller feels negative about Mr. Schulz. Above all, they disturb insulting statements such as: "Well, you're probably not the fastest" or "I think you have to say it all twice until you understand something." She's looking for an interview with Mr. Schulz, he's willing to talk in principle, but he keeps saying in conversation, "I honestly don't even see what a problem you're having. What can be offensive in what I said? "Mr. Schulz blocked by pretending that he did not understand Mrs. Müller's problem. Of course, this turns the discussion into a circle.

- Offensive-Active Procedures

Offensive-Active Procedures include steps as given below:

- Distract (open secondary theatre)

- Fritter Away
- Deliberately Misunderstanding
- Talk a lot, Say Nothing: Throwing smoke candles
- Fake Arguments
- Exaggerate

For example, Mr. Kohn wants to talk to Mr. Mahler's department head about the planned bonus system. In some places, he regards it as unfair and not transparent. However, by engaging Mr. Kohn in a conversation about the new position within his team, Mr. Mahler cleverly distracts from the topic. At the same time, it creates time pressure so that the conversation can end as soon as possible.

- **The Enforcement Strategy**

The manipulator wants to stay in the conversation with the help of the enforcement strategy and attain his goal by all means. The manipulator, that is, he uses claims, false arguments, and persuasive tactics will act convincingly. But he can also pursue a method of enforcement that is not oriented to convictions.

Non–Convincing approaches:

- Selectively Inform
- Threats / Lie / Blackmail
- Personally Attack
- Swinging Emotions up
- Make Fake Licenses
- My Last offer, Then
- Dismissing the item as non-negotiable
- Creates time pressure
- Creates a bad conscience

For example, Max negotiates with his landlord to take over the costs of renovation. The landlord is only willing to pay 2,000 euros, which would be far from covering the costs. Owner: "So I want to tell you one thing: 2,000 euros is my last word. If you don't accept that, then no renovation will happen." The landlord uses the "My last offer" method to put pressure on Max and get Max to give in.

Belief-Oriented Approaches:

- Flatter
- Make concessions on an emotional level, which should contribute to the factual level
- Appeal the Vanity / Prestige
- Authority (Intimidate)
- Unsettle: own solution as a lifeline
- Putting forward false arguments

For example, Mr. Karl and Mrs. Huber address the issue, which deals with the more rational distribution of competencies. Mr. Karl is superior to Ms. Huber. Mr. Karl: "Well, Ms. Huber, I have to say, you're doing an excellent job, it's seriously considered here in the House to consider you at the next promotion round. Especially from the customer side, you hear only positive things. I don't quite understand why you're so busy with this issue of competence..."
Through vague promises and flattery, Herr Karl tries to make Frau Huber "docile." Mr. Karl speculates that Ms. Huber leaves her post.

- **Sabotage in Conversation**

Sabotage in conversation means that the manipulator wants to break the conversation but doesn't want to take responsibility for it.

Typical situations:

- Deliberately Misunderstanding
- Provoke Insult
- Provoke Demolition
- Express Allegation
- To behave uncooperatively (not to be excused)
- Lie
- Let tears flow
- Declare emotional outburst as a legitimate reaction
- Pretend an appointment that you would have forgotten
- Lead / Terminate conversation too fast
- Make the last offer, then
- Dismiss the item as non-negotiable
- Create time pressure
- Create a bad conscience
- Insist on your own point of view
- Deny explanation
- Block information
- Do not answer questions

For example, Paul has a conversation with his team leader Peter. Paul believes that the distribution of teamwork could be more efficient and now wants Peter to talk about how such a distribution of tasks could be addressed.

Peter to Paul: "We will not redistribute the work in our team. We do not need to discuss that. I can tell you in advance that all your attempts to convince me of the opposite will be a futile effort. Everything stays as it is."

Paul: "But there is a possibility, as we still do ..."

Peter: "I do not want to hear anything there; there's just no room for maneuver."

Paul: "But ..."

Peter: "No, Paul."

- **Sabotage after the Conversation**

It is particularly frustrating when the manipulator shows cooperative behavior in the conversation, but after the conversation sabotages and the agreed results, solutions, measures, etc. bring to failure or underrun.

Typical Procedures:

- Reinterpret Agreements
- Agreements simply do not comply
- Rushing and intriguing others
- Build up obstacles and blockades

Here's an example of post-conversation sabotage that reinterprets an agreement.

For example, Mr. Gerber is a project manager in a software project. Ms. Luck is the superior and principal of Mr. Gerber. Mrs. Luck is dissatisfied with the information flow. In an interview on this topic, they agree that Mr. Gerber submits a status report to the project every week.

Although every week Luck receives a report, the information in it is so sparse that she cannot get a clear idea of the status of the project. Mrs. Luck is requesting a statement from Mr. Gerber.

Mr. Gerber: "I assumed that the information should be as short as possible so that you can quickly get an overview."
Mrs. Luck: "But this information is not very valuable."
Mr. Gerber: "Then, I probably misunderstood you."
Whether someone will sabotage after a conversation, of course, is not easy to recognize. You should be careful not to rush to judgment. Therefore, one will have to watch over a slightly longer period of time, as the interlocutor behaves. Above all, it is important that your agreements are as precise and unambiguous as possible. Fixing agreements in writing can be a helpful method.

2.3 Emotional manipulation techniques

This segment addresses several emotional manipulation strategies that include gas lighting, victimization, deception, playing with one's feelings, vulnerability, embarrassment and bullying, and lastly, voice change and word change that further describes love bombing and rage outbursts.

- **Gas lighting**

Gas lighting is a psychological method used to make someone doubt his/her perception of reality. To gain the upper hand, the manipulator questions the validity of your memory and your emotions. Finally, you too start questioning yourself. You have trouble relying on your judgment and may even feel like you're going crazy.

- *How to Stop It*

If you feel your partner is throttling you out, you should take a step back from such a situation and try to look at things from a broader perspective. Seeking a family member, colleague, or someone else's opinion outside of the relationship will help you gain unbiased insight into the truth.

Gas-lighting can be either deliberate or accidental. Determining whether or not your partner has sought to make you question your intuition intentionally is important. Try to have an honest conversation about your concerns, without confronting your partner. This may be considered as a sign of deep emotional abuse if you strongly suspect their gas lighting is intentional.

- **Minimizing and Magnifying**

The manipulator minimizes its shortcomings in this type of emotional manipulation while at the same time magnifying yours. It can be so small as forgetting an item in the grocery store, but your partner will harass you in such a way as to make you feel or act like a failure.

- *How To Stop It*

This is another situation where the outsider's perspective can help you determine the truth. Keep a record of all the things that seem like your partner is minimizing their negative behavior and enhancing yours in a safe spot, either on a private notebook or your phone under a password. No matter how small, record anything that feels important. A trusted friend or a therapist may help you traverse the record and gain perspective.

- **Humiliation and Bullying / Devaluation**

Closely tied to diminishing and magnifying, a partner who humiliates and bullies you, even when it's under the pretext of kidding or teasing, does this to make you feel tiny. You are close enough to an emotionally manipulative partner that they know the weaknesses and insecurities, you possess, and can use them as weapons against you.

Probably a partner who bullies you is dealing with massive insecurity about his intelligence and worth. Individuals such as this also target people nearest to them. They can go from pointing out occasionally something you have done wrong to being constantly critical of your actions.

- *How to Stop It*

You don't have to accept this if you feel like your partner is bullying you. Bullying can be a telling sign of manipulation of the emotion that has escalated into abuse. To talk with a counselor, contact a therapist or the National Domestic Violence Hotline.

- **Playing as Victims**

People who play the victim can never take responsibility for their actions that are negative. If every argument ends with you profusely apologizing while your partner rarely says they're sorry, it's a red flag.

It's important to mention that people who seem to beat themselves or display vulnerability constantly and seek your approval may struggle with mental health issues, such as depression or social anxiety. They are never an excuse for coercion but a clarification. In such cases, the individual may have no intention of manipulating you. It is not up to you, though, to overcome their mental health struggles but rather to help their recovery efforts.

But if someone never takes responsibility for their actions or words, tells others how they were the victim in their lives, and always spins situations to look like the aggrieved party, they use manipulation to avoid taking responsibility.

- *How to Stop It*

Start by catching your partner any time you feel the urge to apologize. Insert a moment of reflection instead of saying that you are sorry, automatically. Is it your fault? Would that merit an apology? If not, then don't give any. Instead, state the facts calmly. If your other half tries to double down and apologize anyway, then the conversation will end.

- Change of voice and change of word

This can be of two forms as discussed below,

- **Love bombing**

The beginning of a relationship is an exciting time, particularly when your interest in love sweeps you off. Love bombing is a form of emotional manipulation, as it initially seems so hopeful and romantic, unlike the other entries on this list. Who wouldn't want an outpouring of compliments, gifts, and affection?

Love bombing refers to someone who worships excessively. Every day the person may show up with lunch at your work or send many romantic lyrics, poetic texts. Love bombing may be a sign of stalking down the road, as the person tries to keep control over his partner.

Love bombing can be considered as a way for the manipulator to finely butter you so that when they manipulate you otherwise, you won't protest. Love bombing often takes place after a period of abuse when an abuser attempts to "atone" his behavior.

- *How to stop it*

Someone who seems to have so much love for you may be hard to question, especially if you feel the very same. However, if you're overwhelmed by the amount of adoration your new partner gets, or if you've found a trend of love bombing accompanied by devaluation, it's time to have a frank talk.

- **Angry Outbursts**

If your partner plays cool most of the time, it could be a form of emotional manipulation to treat you like you're overly emotional, only to explode with anger when you try to get them to open up. Both types of people use their anger to shut down the conversation and regain control when they feel it slipping out of their grasp.

Many of these people have issues relating to anger management. If your partner is one of them, it is their responsibility to manage their anger and to control it. Regardless of how much they could blame you for "pushing them over the edge," they are wrong.

- ***How to Stop It***

Anger from someone else is never your fault or your responsibility, no matter how heated your arguments may be. If your partner is yelling at you, calling you names, or exhibiting aggressive behavior towards you, stay calm and don't reciprocate. Take an assertive stance for yourself. If your partner continues to rage, then immediately end the conversation, even if it means physically distancing yourself from them.

- **Lying**

Predators lie constantly about virtually everything in their lives. They do that to get their victim wrong-footed and confuse them. Lying is one of the manipulation techniques commonly used by psychopaths as they do not have any qualms about it.

- **Guilt-tripping**

Someone who manipulates will often blame their victim by saying they don't care about them, or they're egotistical, or their life is easy. All of that helps keep the person confused and anxious.

- **Recovering Your Sense of Identity after Emotional Abuse**

Being an emotional manipulator's goal can have a significant impact on a person's sense of identity. You may not feel like you can trust yourself or anyone else anymore. Meeting with a therapist is an established way of restoring the sense of confidence and power over your own life. Whether you feel the relationship can be saved and want to pursue counseling for the couple, or whether it's time to move on and talk to a therapist individually.

2.4 Techniques of psychological manipulation

There are many types of manipulative people in general: sociopaths, narcissists, liars or so-called psychological vampires. And their detection is more practical than theoretical. Therefore, it will be easier for you to predict them if you've been a target of them at some point.

The goals of manipulative people, however, can be considered very straightforward, and they follow some pattern. Some of those forms of psychological manipulation include:

- **Eradicating your willpower**

Seeking to sow doubt so you can remain under the "protection" of the manipulator.

- **Destroying your self-esteem**

Getting rid of all that you did or did. Through their critique, they aren't constructive; they're just trying to point out shortcomings.

- **Passive-aggressive revenge**

By avoiding you, they punish you. They push you aside when you need them. Even if you ask them about something, they might not be talking to you.

- **Misrepresenting reality**

They enjoy making people confused and generating claims and misunderstandings, among others. They remain on the sidelines after having generated a controversy, having fun watching others argue.

2.5 How to manipulate others using dark psychology

Want to be really successful in your leadership, relationships, parenting, work, and other areas of life? Then evaluate yourself to decide your current motivation and persuasion tactics. Doing it right brings credibility and influence over the long term. Doing it wrong is something, which leads to poor character, broken relationships, and long-term failure as people will eventually see through the darkness and know your purpose.

Various types of dark psychology and the most commonly used manipulation tactics are discussed below. This will help you to be aware of them and to avoid manipulation.

- **Love Flooding**

Love Flooding occurs when someone is giving you a lot of attention and love. It is often used to overwhelm you with presents, congratulations, touch, attention, and compliments. The more you need to accept this mode of manipulation, the more susceptible you are to that. Once the manipulator has formed a bond with you and developed a dependency on their love and affection, they will then exploit you by removing their love and care.

- **Love Denial**

Attention Withhold and affection are called denial of love. Love Withdrawal means removing love, attention, or affection to get some reaction or behavior. This is a very dangerous tactic for parents to use with their kids. This technique is often used with Love Flooding. However, if the manipulator already has a relationship with the person they are trying to manipulate, they don't have to use love flood.

- **Passive-aggressiveness**

Passive-aggressive behaviors seek to avoid direct confrontation, yet attempt to obtain a particular response. Passive-aggressive tactics include incitement to sarcasm and shame. People who don't want that tactic to be perceived as aggressive or overly assertive use it. People who fear direct confrontation often make use of passive-aggressiveness. See strategies to cause sarcasm and remorse below.

- **Guilty Induction**

Guilty Induction is used by a manipulator to get someone to do something by invoking a sense of guilt or obligation. Guilt inducing is often implicitly passive-aggressive. A person can make a comment as "I'm quite sure that you don't want to help me move,"

- **Sarcasm**

Sarcasm is a manipulator's attempt to get what he/she wants through negative or cutting statements but ends with laughter or saying they're just jokes. Sarcasm is indirect, and a tactic of passive-aggression.

- **Leading Questions**

Leading Questions is a manipulation technique that uses the questioning process to set a standard and obtain commitment. Once the person is given a level of commitment and sufficient "ok" answers, he/she will then ask the victim for a commitment and will appeal to the individual's need to be consistent with their words and actions. This is a tactic that unethical fund-raisers often use. The presentation is a series of questions that will get you to say "yes" as many times as you can, including affirming the foundation's needs, people's needs, your desire to help; then, the final questions will be asking for some money. This will put you in a position where you risk being seen as incompatible with your values, commitments, and assumptions if you say no.

- **Subliminal Influence**

Subliminal influence is a technique that uses visual and auditory stimulation to seed product familiarity, service familiarity, behavior, or creed. Subliminal messages appeal to the parts of your brain that process visually and audibly. It is sensed and processed by your brain but at a subconscious level. While videos that show an image you can't see (according to research,.003 seconds is the standard) have some effect on you, it's quite small. When used as a subliminal prime subliminal influence is most effective.

- **Choice Restriction**

Choice Restriction is used when someone attempts to get you to decide according to their wishes. A lot of sales professionals are taught this technique to increase their sales volume. This tactic is observed during the sales pitch "closing" phase. Typically it is applied to a problem. The salesperson might ask, for example, "When would you like to start, Monday or Wednesday? "And" Will you pay in cash or by credit card? "The idea is to offer only two options and distract you from an alternative option that you wouldn't want to choose from. In the above example, the salesperson hopes to distract you from the choice of "no."

- **Reverse Psychology**

This is a technique involving the advocacy of a belief or conduct that is contrary to the desired one, with the expectation that this approach will encourage the subject of the persuasion to do what is actually desired, which is the opposite of what is suggested.

- **Mind Games**

These Games are psychological techniques used to create a psychological superiority and one-upmanship struggle between humans. These tactics are often employed passive-aggressive behavior to specifically demoralize or disempower the subject of thinking, making it look superior to the aggressor. Mind games can include communication tactics, including semantic manipulation and social embarrassment, too.

- **Brainwashing**

It is a procedure by which a person or group makes use of underhand methods to persuade others to the will of the manipulator.

But where does he avoid truthful persuasion and start brainwashing? Today, there are many methods of persuasion employed, especially in politics. For instance, a simple way to persuade a crowd to follow your instructions is first to state a few things that cause a' yes' response, then add things that are the facts, and at last, suggest them whatever you want them to do.

2.6 Defining desired outcomes

"Give me, with a goal, a stock clerk, and I'll give you a man who will make history. Give me a no-goal guy, and I'll give you a stock clerk."-J.C. Penny Using NLP (Neuro-Linguistic Programming) and well-defined findings to set better targets.

- **What is it that you really want!**

Whether you want to be a party's life or become a billionaire in three years, goals can be used to help you achieve excellence, whatever that means to you.

If you know what you want to do and where you want to go, better maps can be created to guide you, and new, better, faster, or easier ways to get there.

A well-defined result answers the question: "What is it that you really want?"

- **BE-DO-HAVE model**

If you know the" BE-DO-HAVE "model (over HAVE-DO-BE), you know that you first become the kind of person capable of achieving the desired outcome, and then you do the acts that suit that kind of person.

(This is why many people who succeed frequently pursue the philosophy of "fake it until you do it.") The trick to attaining your goals is to identify them.

- **Believable and Achievable**

But you have to describe them in a manner that is reliable and achievable.

According to Denis Watley, "The reason for most people never achieve their goals is that they don't define them properly, or ever seriously consider them to be believable or achievable." Shlomo Vaknin's The Big Book of NLP Techniques, one of the best writing ups of all time on well-defined results, is from the book.

Align Your Values, Your Desires, and you're needs into One Powerful Direction when you align your mind, emotions, and body, in the same guidance, you can make great things happen.

That congruence is a powerful resulting recipe.

It means you think, sound, and do in clear ways that suit what you want to accomplish.

Vaknin writes: "Put your mind into this outcome as if you had accomplished it and open your mind to the importation of that outcome. The time comes before you start investing lots of resources to rework your outcomes.

The procedure to align with your highest goals is to keep your outcome flexible, rework the outcomes as needed, shape the outcome into something even better.

Now you're developing one of NLP's hallmarks, ecology, where all parts of you are in agreement with the outcome, where your desires, values, and needs are all aligned in one strong direction.

With that in mind, we have to look at the trend of well-defined results and how you can set better goals

- **Steps to Set a Better Goal**

Some steps to set up your goals are given below,

- **Step - 1**

<u>**Create a Specific, Positive Goal:**</u>

Start with an eye to the end. What is your desired outcome or vision, which you want to experience?

Consider it real and consider it meaningful.

What would look good, or what scene you see played in the eye of your mind?

Don't dwell on those things you don't want. Do concentrate on what you want. In a positive manner, state your desired result.

Vaknin writes: "State your outcome/goal in concrete, positive terms. Take the time to spell out exactly what you want.

Not a negative target leads you in that positive direction. Evite goals like "I don't want to be a perfectionist. A' not frame' encourages the subconscious mind to create what it is that you think you resist.

If you delete a question and replace it with something resourceful and constructive, what would it be? Describe it. Include all modes of key senses.

- **Step - 2**

<u>**State your results in Terms of Ability, Not Lack of Ability:**</u>

Reflect on what governs you. Don't give away their power. When you rely on other people, you give away your power.

Vaknin writes: "think about it,' I want others to help me.' That is not a well-formed outcome. In fact this way of thinking will stop you from making progress!

It's true that some goals require additional people to support them, but this ambiguous result doesn't tell what you're going to do to get the support and what exactly that support means.

Consider the alternative: I will have developed and used a strategy by the end of the week that will give people a very positive response in this matter. I will continue to improve it until it's very successful.' Remember that your decisions are the basis for the result. Plus, it must be within your remit and ability. Tell yourself or your customer: What would you do to make this happen on your own?

What actions would you take this week to boost your chances?

- **Step - 3**

<u>**Context:**</u>

When describing your outcome, be context-specific. Where do you want to see this happen? When do you want to see this happen? Who do you want to see this happen?

Vaknin writes: "Context generally defines meaning. Describe your well-formed result regarding the environment in which it will be.

Which makes your target more motivational and precise. It also helps ensure you have set an ecological goal. A more well-formed context-related result would be:' I want to make $65,000 in the next 12 months, beginning on July 1st, by selling my NLP expertise to insurance agencies as a sales consultant for their telemarketing team.' Add places, locations, regions, people and their names, a schedule, time frames and more. You're making it real for your brain by making it specific and context related.

Another contextual thought: where wouldn't you want to act on that behavior?

Would you like to play with your children like a child every day, for example, to make them feel more joyful with you?

Amazing..!

But you wouldn't want your spouse to behave the same way in bed, right?

This is why context is vitally important.

You can make a goal of talking to your wife with more passion and sexiness, but if you forget that the context is' with the wife,' you may slip the wrong tonality into talking to your boss.

- **Step - 4**

<u>Sense Modalities</u>:

Bring your target or desired outcome to life by applying all your senses to the picture (see, hear, sound, taste, smell).

This will help you to bring it much more vividly to your mind, and you will actually feel what it would feel to achieve your objective.

This will inspire you and get your subconscious alongside you.

Vaknin writes: "Use your five senses to describe your outcome.

The specific outcome is a well-formed one.

By adding all the senses, you become more specific, and motivational, again. It adds power to your subconscious, constructive approaches.

If you're going to have to use a word like affection, admiration, or passion, be sure to include the senses that shape the emotion.

What does feeling appreciate more from a sensory point of view mean for yourself?

How does he feel' appreciated'?

What body part do you feel it in?

Who appreciates you, and what sort of expression is there on their face?

- **Step - 5**

<u>**Objectives**</u>:

Choose your target in small steps. This makes your goal more actionable, more credible, more attainable, and easier to reach. That will also help build momentum for you.

Vaknin writes: "Degrade your target into achievable goals (pieces), so you'll feel more inspired and solve problems easier.

Make sure you describe the goals in realistic terms. Smaller stages feel more attainable. This adds motivation, which is subconscious. In NLP we call this breakdown' chunking down.'

How do you feel about writing a whole book when you think about it?

Or does he lose 60 pounds?

Compare that to smaller pieces, 'To complete a 240-page book, I'll write a page per day. Today I'm just going to concentrate on that one page.' How do you eat an elephant? One-piece at a time.

- **Step - 6**

<u>**Support**</u>:

Identify the support you need and how you will get that support. Be true.

Vaknin writes: "Arrange the support you need to make the result a reality. What tools is it that you need?

Make a list of the tools you'll be using to achieve your goal.

Let's say team members are an important resource, and persuasive pitch is a resource for acquiring them.

This outcome includes both: 'I will have a complete list of people by the end of the week, who are good candidates for teaming up on the project. I will create a persuasive approach to contact them by the end of the following week, and I will call at least twenty of them. I'm going to continue until I have five trustworthy commitments.'

Again, be specific!

Who are those people who can help?

What are its names?

What are their occupations?

What about their telephone numbers?

What should you ask them, exactly?

Which emotions do you need to grow inside of yourself?

Need more confidence, more resilience, more joy, or more assertiveness?

How much money does it make?

What would be important information? Which questions should be answered in advance?

What else is it that you need?

- **Step - 7**

<u>Perform an ecology check</u>:

Do you want to really achieve this goal?   Are your doubts in second place? Do you experience the internal tugs in a different direction? Are there any disputes you need to resolve?

Find yourself out if anything keeps you off.

Vankin writes: 'What could interfere with your aim? Are there any daunting principles, specific goals, citizens or laws? How can you accommodate or mitigate to make your dream come true now?' Take into account any internal challenges that you might have. Does one part of you interfere with your goal?

- **Step - 8**

Create your milestones:

Break down your target to milestones. Include the milestones into your calendar.

It gives you a way of seeing and enjoying success as you are and helps you stay on track.

Vankin writes: "Determine how you know you are moving at the right pace in the right direction ad.

You need to know what signs of progress you'll observe along the way.

One way of creating achievements is to put the resources on a timeline from your checklist.

Vagueness is a warning sign about milestones.

Mark the dates you'll be checking every milestone on your calendar.

Note exactly what you wish to see in your plan by that date.

It is an awesome goal to be a great lover, but what about learning to read the body language of the person you are with?

That would be an excellent step forward towards your goal. Even a seemingly insignificant thing can be a positive accomplishment.

If you want to get rich, your checkbook balance is part of your master plan, as insignificant as it seems.

- **Step - 9**

Write your goals down:

Writing down your expectations helps strengthen those goals. It also helps you to think about them, and to check how things go. It also helps to keep the mind from spinning stuff around.

Vankin writes: "Writing down your goals, objectives, and milestones has many benefits. Getting a notebook or file for this gives you space for problem-solving and creativity. Sometimes when you later come across it, a misplaced thought turns into a gold mine.

Having separate portions for these elements gives you a working reference to check milestones, refine your objectives, and work towards your goals.

The paper they're written on isn't worth unwritten objectives, but the written word is important.

Isn't it worse having your face on a' Most Wanted' poster than hearing about it?

- **Step - 10**

<u>**Check**</u>:

Take action and test results for yourself. Beware of your results. Your feedback is your result. Make better use of your feedback. "Monitor your progress on the goal and its milestones," Vankin writes: To remind you, keep this in a conspicuous place. Find this pattern anyways has helped you advance towards your target.

Make this pattern for other objectives and to refining them as required.

Note any ways this trend has strengthened your ability to be more mindful of your goals and achievements and to stick to them.

Remember all the challenges you experience and determine which NLP trends you might be able to help with. Part of this pattern's charm is making challenges more visible so you can tackle them. "Additional advice don't compete with yourself. Get on your side by knowing what you want to do, and why. Vankin writes: "It's fairly easy to become a master procrastinator in this modern world with all its technology and comfort.

Just remember to keep the result in mind as a direction and not a list of' to do.' Make it a big result, so it inspires you, and then let it be as you take small steps and celebrate every milestone.

Think of your outcomes not as final outcomes, but as a means of achieving a great and compelling aim. That is a real motivating force.

Which is your project's larger purpose!

Explore its importance before you come into contact with the powers that drive you. In this situation, you'll realize that when that progress feels good, you're making good progress. "That's a pretty detailed look at how to set goals that are believable and attainable.

It's also a great pattern to show where your priorities could fail, either because of alignment, lack of action, or lack of motivation. The larger approach to keep in mind is to keep acting toward your successful scene and remember that there is no failure, only feedback.

Chapter 3: Mind manipulation Facts and Fiction

The theory of mind control is a common one. The ability to influence the free will means a reckonable force. The problem is that the mind control force is prone to exaggeration. Mostly this can be blamed on the tendency of the popular culture to embellish reality with impossible feats. Often these beliefs go beyond logic and cause people to think that control of the mind is a superpower–and thus fiction.

3.1 The Reality of Mind Control

You must first remove any doubts you may have concerning the existence of mind control. It's an authentic practice. Doubting its presence will only make you more vulnerable to its effects, as you won't be able to spot signs of manipulation. Not knowing about the attack means not being able to defend oneself.

Second, you have to realize that some of the theories you think are theoretical about mind control are factual. For example, due to the subtlety of the techniques involved, the effects of mind control, whether done by you or on you, are difficult to spot. Through simple actions such as repeating a word or showing you a specific color, anyone without your knowledge could influence your beliefs. It can even be achieved by merely suggesting that there is something there. You may not have realized yet, but your views on mind control were affected by the two previous paragraphs. Now that you've been told of the attempt, you might doubt the author's validity and the argument–this last sentence also tries to sway your mind and convince you that the book is a sham.

So you can clearly see that influencing a mind is simpler than you might think, especially if the target doesn't know they're under attack–the worst-case scenario. So we have to agree that there is control of the mind.

It is also an established fact that mental control is usually exercised to create dominance over a particular target. For starters, advertisements condition minds to purchase some items or take advantage of certain services. Such ads are intended to stay subconsciously with the viewer: the louder the commercial, the higher its hold. Often, this hold is triggered by proximity to the product itself or situations which may require it. Your subconscious memory tells your conscious mind you need the product and makes you believe the decision was your own. You then buy it or use it, and if the mechanism is triggered again, the cycle repeats.

At some point or another, you'll have witnessed this scenario; at this very moment, you may even be experiencing it. Think about why you prefer a particular brand over their competition or why you like a specific politician better than another, to take the idea even further. You might say it depends solely on your personal preferences, but why do you have those preferences? The decision couldn't have come from anywhere; it started because of the power politicians or corporations have over you. By now, the effect may be so deeply ingrained in your mind that you cannot imagine choosing anything or anyone else.

3.2 The Realistic Scope of mind control

Now it's the time to separate fact from fiction. To better understand this, we'll need to revisit the basics of the psychoanalysis concept of Sigmund Freud. Our use of this field of study may vary somewhat from the usual, by concentrating more on the unconscious's effect on the conscious decisions that you make.

Note, if you will, that psychoanalysis involves splitting the human consciousness into two parts: the conscious and the subconscious. Commonly called the' ego' is the conscious mind. This is the part of one's brain that makes and contributes to all the decisions. The subconscious part of your mind, on the other hand, is itself split into two parts: the 'I d' and the 'superego.' Then 'I d' the raw emotion within you; it is uncontrollable and does whatever it wants, irrespective of the moral consequences. On the other hand, the superego reflects the part of your mind that respects social and ethical norms. This can be considered the most vigilant aspect of your mind because it takes all possible consequences into account.

Let's go back to your conscious mind, your ego. People mostly believe that by consciously analyzing every benefit and consequence of a particular action, you create a choice. Bringing the ego into perspective works in a similar way to the superego. People tend to forget, though, that humans do find the ability to take pleasure from a decision. From this angle, it becomes clear how the Id engages. Hence the ego is your subconscious thinking greatly influences the result of the battle between the Id and the superego and your conscious decisions.

How does this relate to Mind Control truth and tales? To influence or monitor the actions of a person means to be able to manipulate the subconscious mind of that person. This is the real power of the mind.

Trying to manipulate the conscious thoughts of a person with force will cause that person to notice and become defensive. They are often driven into retaliation, which leads to conflict afterward. If you can subconsciously influence that same person, though, he or she will assume that he/she has come to his / her own conclusions. If you return from the previous section of this chapter to the first example, you will notice that every argument slowly guides you toward a particular thought. You must have been thinking for yourself because you read that section actively, but did not every statement cause you to doubt your own stance on the nature of mind control? You may even have been debating the continuation of the book with yourself, as noted earlier.

3.3 Myths about Mind Control

What you now hold is either a book or any device that you use to read. The reality is that you are currently holding or using a tool that attempted mere moments ago to control your thoughts. By contrast, popular culture might also have convinced you of some claim to have outrageous abilities. Remember anything you have heard about mind control beforehand. One or more of the fallacies below may be recalled.

Some claim a form of hypnotics necessarily results in mind control. This is half-true in that you are, in some way, hypnotizing the person while trying to control a person's mind. This isn't the type of hypnosis commonly associated with the word, however. No one who knows your intent willingly allows you to use conventional means to hypnotize him or herself. Stereotypical hypnosis also requires both parties to concentrate, and a quiet environment. A hypnotized person often shows limited cognitive functions to the point of being between wakefulness and sleep. Primarily, the traditional hypnotism picture doesn't work because you end up with an unconscious body rather than an apparently normal behavior or judgment.

Another idea is to be some kind of psychic for the control of minds. This one is an obvious mistake because precise control of the mind does not require supernatural ability. Related to this is the misconception that only people who can use 100 percent of their brains can learn to control their minds. The fact is that everyone actually uses the full capacity of the human brain, not just the 10 percent that is often claimed by popular culture. An open and observant mind is what really matters in learning mind control; not everyone can have one, but everyone can try to develop one. In the later chapters, this will be further emphasized.

Ultimately, there is an idea that because of intense focus, a person who uses mind control can suffer severe headaches and that staring will help intensify the effects. As will be pointed out later, unless you are still in the beginning stages, you do not need to be physically present to control a person's mind. The mere presence of an object or a situation can trigger your control, so you don't really need to keep up with your target all the time. You'll need to concentrate, but not so much so that your veins begin to stick out of your forehead, and your face twists up as if you'd have to poop. Only focus enough to avoid missing anything to help you track your aim.

Chapter 4: Mind manipulation in everyday life

Nobody likes to be manipulated. Whether it's a part of our personal or professional lives, the notion of coercion is usually regarded as evil.

Most of us equate it with negative connotations, like people trying to take advantage of us or forcing us to do something that we really don't want to do.

You are most likely to be manipulated every day, both in your personal and professional life, whether you realize it or not. Everywhere, advertisers and companies accept and harness the power of coercion to get us to buy those things and to live our lives in some way.

4.1 How to Spot a Manipulator

'There are those whose basic ability is to spin the wheels of manipulation. It is a part of their existence, and without these spinning wheels, they simply do not know how to function."

Having discussed the different ways in which people exploit us, it's only fair to educate you next time on how to be more careful. Emotions are what manipulators aim for, as has been shown up to now. We all have feelings, albeit to varying degrees, and for this reason, we are all exposed. Although none of us are immune to manipulations, there's certainly something we can do to make sure we don't fall for them whenever someone tries to manipulate us. This next part will highlight some of the ways that spotting and, hopefully, evading a manipulator can be helpful.

- **Knowing if someone is trying to control our mind**

Maybe it is your loving spouse who you apparently can't ever please or your child who so yearns for that bicycle he's been pestering you about for so long; perhaps it is your local coffee vendor or your or a total stranger who vends his merchandise by the roadside, maybe it is your school principal or your local pastor, possibly your best friend or your arch-nemesis, it is necessary to beware of your associations lest you fall for manipulations. It is important to note, however, that all types of coercion are harmful. As such, not all of them are to be shunned. An example of a useful technique of oppression is when, at school, a parent gives their child something for good grades.

Nevertheless, it is essential to be aware of the motives of other people and to be the final judge of whether or not we wish to continue with a particular course of action. For example, if you are aware that you are being manipulated and yet are okay with it, then, by all means, allow it to continue. The advantage of this is that the manipulation will remain under your own conditions, and you can opt-out whenever you wish. However, the problem is that this may not be taken as manipulation. Some people may argue that the moment the target is aware of the tricks but encourages them to go on anyway, it ceases to be manipulation seeing the situation as if they are going to have a lot more control.

Manipulation, as you must have learned by now, preys upon the emotions of people. There are certain features, as such, that are more likely to be present in a manipulator. This does not mean that these specific features are necessarily references to such men. Instead, they are general, thus playing with the law of averages.

Be very careful when you see one or more of those traits in a person you are associated with. Note that the more of these traits that manifest in a person, the more likely a manipulator is involved with you. The opposite, however, is also quite possible because you can find a person with all of these characteristics and yet are not included in any manipulation. Where possible, this next section outlines and explains the said traits with relevant examples.

- **Traits of Manipulators**

In an effort to find a common pattern, all that has been discussed to this point will be related to the said traits. The dark triad, a combination of which is considered to bring out the best environment for the creation of the most effective manipulators, is three of the main traits that will be addressed. These are; narcissism, psychopathy, and Machiavellianism. The other traits to be mentioned, including charm and nonchalance, are more observations of character than personal traits. Nevertheless, they are also strong indicators for manipulators.

- **The Psychopath**

The word psychopath is a descriptive term for a person who shows a complete lack of empathy towards other people or animals. A person like that will go through life in a way that's completely empty of feelings. For this reason, a psychopath would find it very difficult to develop any real relationships with others. This is because deep attachments involve emotions which a pathological psychopath never considers a strong suit. For them, the main motivation for striking encounters with others would be for convenience purposes only. This means people with psychopathic tendencies are likely only to initiate friendships, acquaintances, or relationships with others when they have something to gain from such arrangements.

The initial description of a psychopath is likely to mislead people into thinking there is no chance of them being psychopaths whenever a person is so deeply engaged with others. This cannot be any further from the truth. Psychopaths can potentially be some of the best actors we've seen. We are able to enter into apparently quite committed relationships and quite quickly tear them apart. Among us, psychopaths masquerade as devoted husbands, loving dads, compliant babies, caring parents, loyal friends, among other highly desirable personalities. These also live on the flip side, as the cold-blooded, cruel, and heartless characters that many people take to be. Psychopathic traits are often hidden in such circumstances, but nonetheless, they exist.

The absence of remorse, guilt, or emotions means that psychopaths can be the most objective people you can find. Not only are they quick to make up their minds, but they are also more likely to stick to a plan once it is settled upon. Such characteristics provide them with the ability to be among the most effective manipulators around. This is because a lack of empathy means that they will settle for the best targets irrespective of how vulnerable they are. Where most people might have ethical dilemmas, psychopaths will sail through quite easily. A good example is if the perfect mark for your guile manipulation is a helpless old lady. The psychopath will settle on the mark without a second thought in which most other people will reconsider their options.

Research shows that many con artists have a considerable amount of psychopathic tendencies. Psychopathy is regarded as one of the qualities that make for a successful con. This is because, for proper manipulation of their targets, cons must not become too attached to their marks lest they start getting concerned about them. If this happens, they may spare them some of the heartless, manipulative tactics, therefore, risking their whole plan. In this situation, a good con man will be able to look you in the eye and promise you heaven as he ushers you through the fiery gates of hell.

- **The Narcissist**

When a person is called a narcissist, it means the person is so self-centered that they blatantly ignore other people's feelings or wellbeing around them. Putting one's own thoughts, desires, and emotions above those of others is a common human trait. Narcissists, though, take self-love to an entirely new level. They disregard other people around them all together and expect others to exalt and praise them. This self-centeredness makes narcissists the objects of other ridicule and scorn. No one loves people blowing their own horns while jumping onto others to hit their destinations.

Narcissists are very competitive people, given their self-centered natures and their insatiable urges for approval from others. More often, they are always willing to do whatever it takes to achieve their goals, even if it means the wrong way for others to be brushing. So it goes without saying that a narcissist will not hesitate to use others to further their egoistic agenda. What's more, they'd do that without showing an iota of remorse for doing so, especially when they get the results, they first wanted to.

There are some traits that predispose people with narcissistic tendencies to manipulate their fellow human beings. Additionally, this includes, but are not limited to, a propensity to live lavishly, an egoistic sense of entitlement, greater self-worth than life, total disregard for others, and unhealthy competition. A closer look at these narcissistic traits reveals that people who exhibit them are more likely to exploit others. For example, the first one is a tendency to live lavishly. For an extravagant lifestyle to be afforded, one must first have the means to afford it. This fact suggests the person must be a great accomplisher and a very ambitious individual. Honest toil alone could afford such a lifestyle but hardly so. Even if it could be done by an honest hard worker, chances are he or she would not live extravagantly. This leaves us with another group of people, the narcissistic ones. A group of people will go to all lengths to maintain their status, including malicious exploitation.

The spotting of narcissistic tendencies in a person is simple. Here, watch out for people who live larger than life and like to rub it in other people's faces, are overly competitive and sometimes unnecessarily competitive, don't care about others' welfare, and are very self-titled. If you can get one or more of these tendencies in a person, it is safe to assume that you are dealing with a narcissist. The chances are that the person will not hesitate to manipulate you if he or she gets a good chance of doing so. It is advised to proceed with caution when you come across such an individual.

- **The Machiavellian**

The Oxford dictionary defines a Machiavellian as a person who would try to achieve their goals by cunning, scheming, and unscrupulous methods.' The term originates from Nicola Machiavelli's description of how effective leadership should be. In his description, Machiavelli argued that an efficient prince should use fear, deceit, cunning, ruthlessness, and duplicity if he was to govern his subjects properly. For the purposes of our discussion, it is clear that a person with Machiavellian traits fits our idea of the manipulator. The very definition of the term qualifies him as so. A Machiavellian is a pathological and compulsive liar who would lie to you about anything and everything.

Like the other two dark-triad traits already discussed, there are signs to look out for if you may want to determine whether or not a person is Machiavellian. The first and most obvious from the definition given is if the person is an impulsive liar. This makes for one of the main qualities required out to carry out a manipulative scheme. This is because, in order to effectively manipulate someone into doing something, the person being targeted must not suspect a thing. One of the manipulator's main goals must, therefore, be to hide his true motives. As such, they are lying forms an essential part of the manipulation. It is important to know that lying doesn't just come naturally for everyone. Whereas others may be perfectly comfortable with deceiving others even regarding very important things, others will find it very hard to lie about the smallest and irrelevant pieces of information. However, deceit is a learned trait and can develop over time. For someone to be classified as a Machiavellian, he or she must have honed the art of lying convincingly over a long time.

A close consideration of deceit reveals that, at its most basic form, it is a form of manipulation. After all, why do people lie? Just for the fun of it? I doubt it. Lying is done to mislead people or to shield them from the truth. Either way, it still qualifies as a manipulation. To explain, consider both uses of lies. If it is used to mislead people, the culprit is manipulated into believing that something is true when it is not or that something is false when, in fact, it is true. The agenda for this first use may be to drive the deceiver's personal agenda or to harm the unsuspecting victim. A well-executed lie and a well-crafted manipulation tactic, in this sense, are one and the same. The other stated use of lying to shield people from the truth is also a form of manipulation.

Another common characteristic of Machiavellianism is aggression. Machiavellian people may be aggressive as a result of trying to get their lies to stick. At one specific point or at another point, we all have come across those people who tend to get aggressive, loud, or even violent for no good reason. They behave in this manner, especially when they are doubted in any manner or when you express your reservations about what they say. With the aim of preventing you from following this course of action, such individuals fly off the handle and react in various unpredictable ways. Your attention ends up shifting from the main point (their lies) to their actions, which have sharply changed for no apparent reason.

Like was the case with the other dark-triad traits, it is clear that Machiavellianism is a strong indicator of the propensity towards psychological manipulation. Likewise, it is very easy to spot someone with this tendency. As stated, the main indication for a Machiavellian person is the tendency to lie, which is higher than that of the average person. In addition, they lie with such confidence that it is so easy to believe them. If you have a friend who falls under this category, beware because the chances are that you are being taken for a ride. Another pointer is aggression, particularly designed to avert attention or to change an uncomfortable topic. These are the telltale signs of a Machiavellian, and it is advisable to proceed with caution when you observe them in someone.

• Nonchalant Person

Nonchalance is indifference to situations, events, consequences, or individuals. From the face value, nonchalance seems hard to be a trait you might find in a manipulative person. Nonetheless, it is one, and here is an example of why. Melvin is a vintage car enthusiast, and more recently, a dealer. At any given time, you will find the upwards of ten vintage cars in his compound. Nevertheless, he is not one to advertise his cars as do other car dealers, which also serves his purpose as his main passion is to collect vehicles rather than sell them. Each day, he spends several hours polishing each and every one of them and then fine-tuning them to make sure they're in peak form.

One day after a neighbor who had been harassing him with a request to buy one of his vehicles for a long time made one final offer, he developed an interest in turning his passion for profiting. The car Mr. Shaw was interested in was a 1965 Mustang, classic yellow. One morning as Melvin went about his business of washing his cars, Mr. Shaw came in and told him he would pay for the vehicle a hundred thousand. At first, Melvin thought he didn't listen well to his neighbor. "And forgive me? "He was wondering. "One hundred thousand dollars. Do you want to take it? "The deal has been made yet again. He would, of course, take it. Mr. Shaw had more than doubled his highest offer yet, and nearly five times the price Melvin paid for, it was one hundred grand.

The first few times, Mr. Shaw offered to take the mustang out of Melvin's possession; however much he insisted he had been met with sincere indifference. Melvin just wasn't ready to part with his car. Such nonchalance on the part of Melvin forced his neighbor to bid an obscene amount for the car that he so wished to own. His second sale was also so lucrative as first he had no desire to sell. The customer kept upping their bid until finally, he could no longer resist it. Of course, such a business approach won't work all the time. It's going to backfire at times, but

Melvin was well prepared for that. After all, he fulfills his other passion for collecting when he is not making a lucrative sale.

The above definition takes nonchalance as an' expression' of coercion. But genuine nonchalance can also be a powerful instrument of manipulation. This is particularly since it implies that the individual could not really care less about the outcome of a given situation. Take, for example, two of your roommates. If one actually doesn't matter if the room is clean or not, doing all the cleaning is incumbent on the other. In this way, nonchalance helps one to take advantage of the other, and thus counts as an example of coercion. How one can get out of a situation like that is clear.

- **The Charismatic**

We have all met people whose mere existence is larger than life. They talk big, and their messages about the future are always hopeful. Charismatic individuals have in their wake many followers who treat every word that comes out of their mouths as truth. We have faith in all they do and are often seen as innovative and progressive people.

Humans have evolved over time to evaluate things or people accurately using their face values to save time that may be needed to examine every situation and every person in detail. Imagine, for example, that you're lost in a town and are searching for someone to ask for directions. There are two people you can take your directions from. A tattooed biker with a long scar running the length of his face is the first person. With his bike by the side, he leans on a lamp post and has a cigarette stuck between his lips. The second person is a security guard leisurely dozing off outside a store in his chair. Which of those two would you choose to ask for directions? A lot of people would go with the security guard even though you might have to wake him up from his sleep uncomfortably.

It is more of the same thing with charm and charisma but on an even bigger scale. People with charisma often rise to the zeniths of the career paths they have chosen without trying as much as the average person would. It is for this purpose that charismatic people are popular at the helms of different institutions, companies, and governments. Often their mere presence is enough for such individuals to sway crowds however they wish. This is because they inspire and command respect, and the majority of people are inclined to trust them. Charisma doesn't necessarily mean something bad. But it becomes an issue when people take advantage of their magnetism. It is just wrong to use superficial charm and empty promises to advance one's personal agendas.

It is important to note that the manipulators often do not show the features discussed in singularity. You will find, in many cases, that a person exhibits a multiple of these traits at one go. It goes without advising that the more you observe such traits in a person, the greater the chances that you will be dealing with a manipulator.

4.2 Victims of manipulation

The ultimate victim can have many benefits, being or even seeming to be. The survivor is safeguarded from attacks from others, one way or another. I also have the compassion and understanding of many, no matter what they're doing. In fact, anyone who dares to question an alleged victim's actions is deemed to be disrespectful or callous.

In many cases, victimization is a strategy that represents more advantages than problems. This condition allows for a kind of security that all they say is true, all they do is with good intentions, and all they believe is real. But in more than one situation, it consciously or unconsciously conceals extortion from that calculated victimization.

- **The Victims**

There are, of course, real victimization situations like when someone has been subjected to abuse or excess, without having had an opportunity to react. For example, when someone is attacked on the street or harassed by someone else who holds power over them, they cannot overcome them: the power of a weapon, uniform, place, etc.

Such situations trigger an objective victimization condition. But this condition is not built-in, nor should the person carry a seal wherever they go. We proceed with the position of the victim as a choice after leaving the particular situation of powerlessness, not a finite reality.

One thing is certain a victim needs care, compassion, encouragement, and affection. To leave their state of shock and insecurity, they need commitment and understanding. Can't argue this.

What's open to debate is the existential position of victimhood. A traumatic event transforms into an eternal cover letter. And not only to bear witness to an execrable fact but also to gain privileges that would otherwise not be obtained.

These are the kinds of people who guarantee the careful display of their misery on their living resume.

Some think that being victims of a situation, in more serious cases, gives them carte blanche to hate or hurt others.

- **Recognizing the Victimizing Manipulator**

Some signs exist of those who manipulate by playing the victim. The most significant ones are:

- The victim does not directly ask what they want, but rather in the form of a question or regret sends misleading messages. They say to you, for example, suddenly: "Nobody knows how hard it was for me to get here." Then you don't know if they want you to recognize their merit if they complain because it wasn't as hard for you, or if they want you to help them with something in particular.

- When you are with this person, you feel more or less guilty. Each interaction that you have with them leaves you with the feeling that you are responsible for something, but you can't define it. There's a sadness with you or a vague discomfort

- The survivor is also distrustful and suspicious. Sometimes they warn you about other people's bad intentions and explain their misdeeds through their past sufferings. They can personally accuse you of callousness or apathy if you contradict them by chance.

- We will make great sacrifices for others without asking them. They're going to show off over it. When someone displays these traits, we deal with a person who has assumed the role of victim to life. It is definitely someone who is not pleased to be in that role and who has such actions without actually trying to do it.

Whatever the case may be, it's someone who failed to complete the process of their traumatic experiences. They need your understanding, but they need your sincerity as well.

The best manner to help someone like that is by politely and specifically asking them what you think about their attitude

- **How to Recognize Mind and Emotional Control and Deception**

If you ever felt like something is off in an intimate relationship or casual encounter— you're being manipulated, controlled, or even feeling like you're questioning yourself more than usual— it could be manipulation.

"Manipulation is an emotionally destructive psychological strategy employed by individuals unable to ask directly what they want and need," says Sharie Stine's, a California-based therapist specializing in violence and toxic relationships. "People who try to manipulate others try to control others." There are many different forms of manipulation, from a pushy salesperson to an emotionally abusive partner — and some behaviors are easier to spot than others.

Here, experts explain the telltale signs that the subject of manipulation could be you.

- **You feel Obligation, Fear, and Guilt**

The concerned manipulative behavior involves three basic factors.

According to Stine's:

Fear, obligation, and guilt are the basic factors. "When you are being manipulated for something, by someone, you are psychologically coerced into doing something you may not want to do," she says. You might feel scared to do these things, obligated to do it, or guilty about not doing it.

She points to two common manipulators: "bully" and "victim." She says a bully makes you feel scared and may use aggression, threats, and intimidation to control you. The victim instills a sense of guilt in their target. "Usually, the victim does hurt," Stine says. But while manipulators always play the victim, she adds that the fact is they're the ones that caused the problem.

A person targeted by manipulators who play the victim often tries to help the manipulator to stop feeling guilty, says Stine's. Victims of such kind of manipulation often feel responsible for helping the victim to stop their suffering by doing whatever they can.

● Questioning yourself

The word "gas lighting" is often used to describe deception that causes individuals to doubt themselves, their reality, memory, or thoughts. According to Stine's, a manipulative person can twist what you're saying and make it over them, seize the conversation or make you feel like you've done something wrong when you're not quite sure you've done it.

If you're being gas lighted, you may feel a false sense of guilt or defensiveness — like you totally failed or had to do something wrong when, in fact, Stine's says, that's not the case.

"Blame the manipulators," she says. "We don't take responsibility."

● Strings Attached

"If you don't get a favor just because, then it's not' for fun and for free,'" Stine's says. "If the strings are attached, then there is manipulation." Stine's refers to one type of manipulator as' Mr. Nice guy.' This person could be nice and give other people plenty of favors. "It's very frustrating because you don't know anything that's negative," she says. "But, on the other end, there is a string attached to every good deed — an expectation." If you don't meet the expectations of the manipulator, you'll be made to be ungrateful, Stine's says.

In reality, one of the most common forms of manipulation is to manipulate the norms and expectations of reciprocity, says Jay Olson, a Ph.D. researcher studying manipulation at McGill University.

For example, a salesperson might make it look like you should buy the product because he or she gave you a deal. A partner in a relationship may buy you flowers and then ask for something in return. "These tactics work because it violates social norms," Olson says. "Reciprocating favors is natural, but even if someone does one insincerely, we often still feel compelled to reciprocate and obey."

- **You see the 'Foot-in-the-Door' and 'Door-in-the-Face' techniques**

Manipulators frequently pursue one of two methods, Olson says. The first is the technique of foot-in-the-door or, in which someone begins with a small and reasonable request— like, do you have time? Which then leads to a bigger request, like I need 10 dollars for a taxi. "That's commonly used in street scams," says Olson.

The door-in - the-face technique is the opposite, it involves someone making a large request, rejecting it, then making a smaller one, explains Olson.

For example, someone doing contract work may ask you for a large sum of money upfront, and then ask for a smaller amount after you've declined, he says. This works because, according to Olson, the smaller appeal seems comparatively reasonable following, the larger request.

- **Signs of manipulation**

Our society romanticizes manipulative connections when thinking about love, so much so that it can be harsh to recognize them for what they are. We have lots of literature suggesting that genuine relationships are about fixation, that pure love is all-expensing, and that infatuated individuals have no boundaries or separate lives.

You may have been warned about manipulative people, and the fact that control and maltreatment is something to worry about; the facts are that being in a relationship of control and manipulation that never grows into ill-treatment can also be frightening and harmful. Just because someone isn't hurting you physically doesn't mean you can't still feel pain from their actions.

Indications of a damaging relationship may be familiar to you. You may have met a partner, for example, who required you to wear only certain clothing items, or did not want you to visit your friends and family.

This person might want to know where you're going, what you're doing and why you're just a couple of minutes late. Manipulators are often very anxious people, allowing nervous thoughts to invade their brains and control their actions. They are going to spiral their excessive emotion and anxiety into fantasies about what you might be doing if you are not around them. They'll think about their worst fears, and what you could do to hurt them, so they'll assume you're doing these things when you're not around.

This can make them dislike you if you're not around. Sometimes it can seem overwhelming to have someone so concerned about you. You might think, "It's so nice that they always want to know where I am, and I'm safe," but this isn't their goal when someone is going to take great measures to control you. Their concern, unfortunately, is not for your wellbeing. Perhaps, they're thinking, "I need to make sure I know where this person is all the time, so they don't do anything I don't approve of."

Your presence is actually their assurance that you're not meeting their worst suspicions about the bad things you're doing to them when you're not the two of you together. In the concerned situation, they are not going to be considerate of your needs. The manipulator acts only to serve his or her own interests.

A manipulator will never tell you that and instead will only be worried about improving the way they look to you. They will use that tactic as well to make sure you feel guilty. We would make you feel guilty when you don't respond for 20 minutes, rather than admitting that it's totally acceptable for a person not always to write back immediately. They will treat you as if you did something wrong or immoral to them, without considering the fact that at the time you were actually not around your phone or too busy to respond in the first place.

Loving should feel better, not confining, scary, or distressing, and to have an accomplice will make you happy, not sadder. There will certainly be troubled times in love. You may not understand your friend, and maybe they don't understand you. These challenges should be mere obstacles to strengthening yourself. A healthy relationship shouldn't be one that continually hurts you and tears you down, making you feel drained all the time.

How manipulators control their victims:
According to Braiker, manipulators control their victims using ways as given below,

- **Positive Reinforcement**

Including praise, superficial charm, superficial sympathy (crocodile tears), excessive apologization; money, gifts, approval, attention, public recognition, facial expressions; as a forced smile.

- ## **Negative Reinforcement**

Involves nagging, yelling, silent treatment (sulking), bullying, threats, cursing, emotional blackmail, guilt trapping, sulking, crying, and victim playing.

- ## **Sporadic or Partial Reinforcement**

Partial or sporadic negative reinforcement, for example, in terrorist attacks, may create an efficient climate of fear and doubt. Partial or sporadic positive reinforcement may motivate the addict to continue-the gambler is likely to win now and again in most forms of gambling, for example, but still lose money overall.

- ## **Traumatic one-trial Learning**

Using verbal abuse, explosive anger, or other intimidating behavior to establish dominance or superiority; even one incident of such behavior may condition or train victims to avoid upsetting, to confront, or contradicting the manipulator.

What can you do if you think you're being manipulated by others?

The way you react to manipulation largely depends on what kind of manipulation you face.

If someone you know or you are in a coercive or even abusive relationship, experts suggest seeking treatment from a therapist or from groups such as the National Domestic Violence Hotline. A good support network, Stine's says, will help too. "People in toxic relationships need somewhere to hear counterpoints. They're conditioned to believe that the interactions are normal. Someone has to help them breakthrough that assumption.

Stine's advises attempting not to let the deceptive actions affect you personally for other kinds of coercion. "Use the motto'

Watch not ingest,'" she says. After all: "We are not responsible for the feelings of anybody else." Also, setting boundaries will play an important role in holding bullying at bay. "Those who exploit have pitiful limits," says Stine's. "As a human being, you have your own volitional experience, and you need to know where you end up and where the other person begins. Manipulators often have either too rigid boundaries or too enmeshed boundaries. "According to Olson, it can also help delay your response in a manipulative situation. For instance, refrain from signing a contract at first glance, do not make a large purchase without thinking through it, and the first time they are brought up, he suggests, and avoid making major relationship decisions. Sleeping on it'" is often the best solution to avoid manipulation," adds Olson.

4.3 Possibility of counterattack

It is only possible to counterattack a manipulator if you have already released yourself from his or her hold. It may take some time to be totally free, depending on the depth of its hold over your subconscious mind.

In this section, the steps you'll learn are easy to perform once you can avoid any attempt to control your mind. You can still use the same move to launch your own attack if you are not yet under attack but want to have an advantage over your competition.

From this point on, it's recommended that you view each chapter as a combat planning. You're going to become a follower of the great strategist Sun Tzu. The stakes in struggle for free will are high.

- **Knowing the Enemy**

The first necessary step in any war is knowing the enemy, according to Sun Tzu's Art of War. This is very important as every single detail about your enemy is critical to a successful battle.

The conscious mind makes decisions based on an id-superego dispute. Knowing which of the two parts dominates in the minds of your target is the key to formulating the perfect attack on him or her.

To know him or her better, it's important that you observe as much as possible of his or her actions. Don't misunderstand this step; it doesn't mean you need to monitor your rivalry around the clock. Only in the "battlefield," you need to watch him or her because this is the only way you want to influence your enemy. You need to pay the most of your attention to the habits and mannerisms of your target. This will reveal a great deal of his or her personality.

On the other side, say your target has a desk that is somewhat cluttered. Many would believe that such a person does not especially value cleanliness, but it is important to know that there are more active minds of people who can work in such an environment. They're flexible enough to work whatever the circumstances. This type of person could, therefore, be more difficult to deal with. Disruption would not be an effective attack; that would require a different approach.

When you find yourself dealing with a strong-minded person, you'll need to go further to weaken his or her defenses. Many specifics are about to come into play. There are certain periods of doubt, even for the strong-willed. Obviously, this also refers to performing a specific task.

The key is to find the right topic or task. Once that awkward subject is found, you can start your attack. This step requires a number of conversations or encounters between you and the target, but once your target attempts to end it, you should never insist on continuing a conversation or a task. So do that will draw attention to what you're doing and cause your opponent's defenses to increase. Be as casual as can be.

A person can exhibit discomfort with a subject or task through other body language types. The person may start scratching his or her head, playing with his or her fingers, pinching his or her nose, or doing anything beyond the usual demeanor, for example. Each person is different, so you need to really observe him or her. Comfort may also be triggered by interaction with a particular object, circumstance, or color.

• Knowing Your Capabilities

You need to know how you are capable of handling your target encounters. As described above, to gather useful information, you'll need to share multiple moments with the target.

Start with showing up. Look in the mirror at yourself, and see if you can be intimidated. If you can do that, you either have a strong personality or are weak enough to be afraid of your own reflection. In order to determine what is true in your case, it is best to practice with a person you know (but of course, not the target. You can do this by slightly altering your look through products and clothes that will catch the attention of your target. For example, if you noticed that your target likes the color pink but hates the color red, wear something that has pink on it and hold something red like a handkerchief (or wear it). As always, don't overemphasize yourself to the point of giving up.

Rest assured, confidence will demonstrate to your target that you are a reckonable force. If you can do so, the target will either keep a close eye on what you are capable of or stay as far as possible out of the way. If the target opts for the former option, you'll need to continue to flaunt your confidence in front of it. Lowering your guard means you're open to counterattacks. Know how well you can hide your real intentions. Note that this whole war needs you to be as calm as possible. Measure yourself by starting a conversation with someone and leading the conversation slowly so that your partner agrees. A good way to practice is by trying to get a girl or a guy that you've just met. If you can pull it off without scaring the guy, you should be ready to commit to your goal.

See how eloquent you can be too. While you don't really need to be an expert in this, it can't be denied that a certain amount of charisma makes it easier to gather information. You need to know how long a conversation can last without becoming repetitive. This is important as the repetition of words gives the impression that you are trying to extend the conversation or mask as intellect a lack of knowledge.

Then, take a look at how well you can keep together. The goal is your competition to some extent; you might even be holding some hostile feelings. Even if remaining under your control is weak enough, he or she might say or do something that gets on your nerves. The worst possible mistake is to lose your calm in the middle of that step. If you find yourself in a situation where you're about to give in to emotion, get back off.

Now that you are conscious of your abilities, it's time to improve them. The most important thing to remember about that is that you need to stop procrastination. Convincing yourself to do this will make you miss your golden opportunity some other day. Learn to avoid procrastination, and each time you compete with your opponent, you'll get ahead.

• Knowing the Battlefield

It's time to consider your battleground. Keep in mind that you are probably not the only people in the area and the target. The collateral damage must be avoided as much as possible. Depending on the battlefield, the solution will be different.

Second, you need to note that to win a fight, you have to have the higher ground. In other words, you always have to look for an advantage. For example, if you want your target to be at ease while you're trying to gather information, try starting a conversation or doing an open space job with him or her. A simple lack of confinement will go a long way towards subconsciously making your target more comfortable with you. Confront the target in a confined space where the only way for him or her to escape is through you if you want to exercise authority. Do not move the space toward the target. Look for the right timing to give it a natural feel. Until it's too late, the target will not know his or her condition, causing immunity.

Third, both you and your target need to know all possible escape routes. In this case, an escape route in any way that anyone involved can avoid an encounter. Do not, therefore, attempt to engage your goal in elevators, doorways, staircases, or any place that offers an easy excuse for stopping the approach. Likewise, if you are the target and want to escape your foe, make use of the places mentioned to cut short the encounter.

Finally, your turf needs to be established. For example, if you're in your office, your desk is your territory. If you're playing a sport, you're happiest in your home area. Never allow the goal in your home turf to gain an advantage over you. If he or she can do that, then you've failed. The ultimate aim is to extend your territory until the whole field is yours slowly. To do so, you have to win battle after battle outside of your own territory until you reach the home field of the target. The final battle will define your supremacy in the one position it is most comfortable with.

To plan for an attack successfully, all three things must be done simultaneously. Know you are still in the process of planning. The next step is where you'll get blood drawn. It's time to strike first.

4.4 Six Maxims for Manipulation Handling

The maximums used for manipulation are discussed below,

- **Stay Factual and Fair**

Look for real arguments and valid justifications, both when you argue for yourself and when your interlocutor bears the burden of evidence, and it is your duty to reason.

- **Stay Calm and Relaxed**

Of course, it's easier said than done. But if you focus on a few basic methods that we'll introduce to you in this book, you'll find it easier.

- **Do not act causally, but Act**

When we are manipulated, we usually show traditional defensive reactions: the manipulator is unfair or emotional, so we too are unfair or emotional, but often we also escape and give in according to the situation. But the manipulator speculates exactly on those reactions-consciously or unconsciously. Basically, there is a kind of stimulus-response mechanism happening in a successful manipulation. This strategy is to break through to retain control of the conversation.

- **Persistently Pursue your Goal**

Be careful not to take the lead; follow your objectives with a bit of tenacity if necessary. Don't be sad. Before the interview, it is best to formulate a clear goal for yourself, which you can always keep in mind.

- **Focus on Concrete Behaviors**

Don't make the mistake of viewing the actions you perceive as the conduct of a certain type of person like "He's just a difficult person," "That's just a mimosa." You're already sorting and analyzing all of your assumptions with such typing. They rush into a trap. This will give you opportunities to have constructive discussions. Looking for concrete behaviors is better, and if you're bothered by that behavior, say so. "Mr. Miller Three times in a row you cut me off."

- **Build a Golden Bridge**

Search for ways the discussion will take a course leading to concrete solutions again. Offer your interlocutor such a possibility, even if he has misjudged it.

4.5 Factors affecting the effectiveness

Many destructive effects of mind control are proportional to:

- The methods used
- The number of techniques
- If hypnosis and/or hypnotic mental control are used
- How often the person is subjected to it and how long

- How close the individual is to the cultivator, how much direct contact there is
- The manipulator's skill
- How much access to the outsiders?
- Presence of sexual abuse
- In one-on-one cult

For example, a situation of a husband and wife in an intimate relationship with a sociopath, where all of the attention is given to a single victim, the results can be very disturbing. Complex trauma is the term used to explain what happens to children raised by psychopathic or narcissistic parents nowadays.

4.6 A growing problem

Issue With the state of the world as it is today, it seems that increasing numbers of people are turning to religious ideas to try to find order or stability in today's turmoil. That means they are more susceptible to cult recruitment because cult offers simple solutions to the difficult problems of life.

In difficult times cult tends to thrive, whether the group is based on religion, politics, finance (making money), fitness, e.g., yoga cult, health, or personal development.

It also seems like more and more horror films are being made today, and that doesn't mean movies with a cult following. There are more and more films about mind control, psychopaths, and malicious sects if you know what you're looking for!

Chapter 5: NLP

5.1 What is NLP

Neuro-Linguistic Programming is a way of influencing the thinking and behavior of people. It emerged in the 1970s after Richard Bandler and John Grinder discovered they would be able to connect neurological processes as well as language to get specific behavioral changes they wanted.

Let's break down the jargon to better understand what NLP is.

Neuro refers to how our brain works. It covers all aspects of our brain, including the cortex, cerebrum, and brain stem. The cerebrum also has two distinct parts, the right, and the left. These are all unique to our biology first, and the genetics we carry with us. Our brain forms are also greatly affected by the experiences we have gone through and the lives we have lived through. Though we can change the way we think, it takes a little longer to influence the way our brain works. Your neurology provides insight into how the way your brain functions can be modified.

Finally, programming refers to the way you were actually "programmed." You were wired a certain way when you evolved into the person you are now. NLP will be all about how you can reprogram yourself, so you think some way. You can use these programs on your own, but they are also useful tools when you influence others too.

Neuro-linguistic programming is a mental technique that declares that methods used by effective people can be modified to achieve one's very own goals. It leads the person to glean from their very personal encounters of achievement and disappointment to identify which processes of thought, sentiments, and practices are helpful. Any action is negative, irrespective of whether it is causing obvious distress as it is only a stage in the learning process.

NLP bases some of the convictions behind the practices on the fact that we can predict some degree of certainty in how humans respond. Given any variations they may have, several people would behave in similar ways to one another.

NLP management is based on the idea that we can predict what might happen in our minds by playing a scenario as we would expect it to happen. From there, we can better understand the potential consequences, understanding what methods of persuasion will work best for achieving the scenario we want.

NLP tactics surround ideas that are based on what we perceive from the world based on what we have been taught in different academic and professional institutions. -map of our society is exceptional, special, and includes changing aspects of what can be assumed to be real.

As one's NLP skills grow, they can better acknowledge the framework that other people use to make decisions. The more you can understand, the easier it is to change the mind of the individual and, in turn, the way they make decisions.

5.2 How others are Using NLP on You

Meta-Communication is a method by which a person gives vague allusions and signals using nonverbal prompts. For example, if a man asks if his partner is okay and she responds "Yes" with a sigh and a shrug on her shoulders, this indicates unmistakably she's not okay, but her verbal response is absolute.

NLP isn't something that'll always be clear. Anyone who uses NLP is typically a practitioner who has regularly applied this technique. Some warning signs might include special attention being paid to you, feeling like you've found your perfect partner, or being flawlessly synchronized with the person you've met quite recently. Look out for someone who's continuing to reflect your non-verbal communication or using ambiguous expressions. It may not bode well for them.

An NLP client will give close consideration to your eyes at the underlying phases of compatibility acceptance. You may think this is because they are seriously motivated by what you say. They are instead watching innovations in your eyes to see how you store and access data.

They'll be able to tell when you're lying or behaving intentionally in no time. They will also be able to identify which parts of your brain you use when speaking.

These individuals learn from what they see you are doing, and from your perspective, they may seem to have an in-depth knowledge of how you feel and what you think. A clever hack for this is to dash your eyes around haphazardly, jump the right, back to the other side, side to side, up-down. Make it appear natural and still do it arbitrarily. This will drive a person NLP crazy as you will distract them from their studies.

One of the essential strategies made use of by NLP specialists is the dubious language to prompt an entrancing daze. The more obscure the word is, the more it drives individuals into a trance, on the grounds that there is less of an individual being subject to differing with or responding to it. On the other hand, explicit language will eliminate the stupor from a single individual.

Make sure that you are also taking care to control language. "Don't hesitate to unwind." "You can test driving this vehicle on the off chance you like." "You can appreciate it as much as you can imagine."

Continuously state, "Would you be able to clarify what you mean?" This accomplishes two things: it interferes with this whole procedure, and it moves the discussion into explicit language, breaking the stupor-inducing use of ambiguous language.

Individuals who use NLP will use vocabulary that has veiled or complex consequences. For example, "Diet, healthy living and submit yourself to me are the most vital things, wouldn't you say?" Superficially, if you heard this sentence spoken quickly, it would appear to be an undeniable articulation that you would presumably concur with unthinkingly.

Indeed, diet and healthy living are, beyond any doubt, critical things. What is the layered-in message, in any event? "The most important items are diet, safe living, and submitting yourself to me, wouldn't you say?" That's right, so you just unintentionally consented to it. With this type of thing, talented NLP specialists can be bold.

Be exceptionally vigilant about daydreaming around NLP people— it's an encouragement for them to jump in with an unnoticed trigger. Here's an example: An NLP client who was trying to get you to write for free for his blog found you didn't put a lot of effort into the work.

If you wind up being directed to settle on something quickly and feel controlled, leave the circumstance. Hold 24 hours before any decisions, especially monetary ones, are settled. Try not to get swept into a decision off the cuff. Sales reps are specifically fitted with NLP systems to plan spur-of - the-moment transactions. Try not to go about it. Don't let yourself be manipulated and hold authority over your life.

Therefore, the preeminent and necessary standard: go with your instincts if you feel someone is manipulating you or you feel the person is trying to manipulate you. Individuals in the NLP appear quite often dodgy. Escape, or let it be known they shouldn't use NLP techniques on you while talking to you.

5.3 Practical Steps to Attain These Skills

Now that you understand what it might look like if someone uses NLP on you, it's time to see how you can use it on others. Just like all other methods of persuasion we've discussed so far in this book, make sure you don't use that in a harmful way. Instead of trying to trick people into doing what you want, use these powerful practices to ensure you both find a place of happiness.

First, let's start by looking at the simple language you are allowed to use. There are seemingly unlimited terms that we can use, and as someone who wants to influence others, you need to make sure you are aware of the common ones used in the strategies of the most highly qualified NLP influencer. The first word is, "don't." Usually, when someone says, "don't look over here," the first thing you want to do is look where they said they did not. This is because our brain does not recognize that "don't." Rather, it only focuses on the actual subject of the conversation, which is the sight that exists within the space that you were told not to look at.

If you want someone to do something for you, first, you might say "don't," but only in a tiny setting. "Don't worry about it right now," is a good thing to say if you really want to talk about something for the guy.

The strongest term that an NLP master can use is "you." When you can make comments about "you or me," it lets the other person imagine themselves. The key to getting anybody to listen to you is thinking about them! People just love to talk about themselves as selfish as it might sound. This is because they are who they are, and the essence of how they perceive the world.

One strategy of the NLP is to use "because," "but," or other explanatory terms. If you were to tell your parents or partner something like, "I need five dollars," they might just think nothing of it and not want to give you the money. If you say, "Because I want to buy some food, I need five dollars," then they are more likely to give you the money, just as simple as that.

Position yourself in their shoes forever. What could hold them up concerning your request? Why would they say no? Look at the part of their brain from there, the reasoning capacity, which will appear when they start making those decisions. You can then look effectively at the vocabulary required to influence their behavior.

5.3 Using NLP for effective leadership

Now that you understand the most basic elements involved in NLP tactics, it's time to look at how these strategies can be used to become an effective leader. It can be necessary to influence people in your daily life, but when you are in a position of power or at least want to be, you need to figure out the balance of authority and control.

A powerful leader knows how to support but not necessarily dominate their followers. How can your decisions affect your lives and those people who love you and listen to you?

Make sure, above all, that you care about your business. Whatever it may be, you are the leader of, you must believe in it and truly understand how it can allow you and your followers to live a better and happier life properly. If you're not involved in what you're doing, then why else?

We've all had times when we're less passionate than others, but as a leader, you must never display this. Just make sure you're confident in your job and committed to it. If you don't put these basic efforts out there, you can't expect anything more from people.

First, make sure you communicate effectively with your squad. Have regular meetings and review cycles and allow them the opportunity to voice any concerns that they might have. When you are unavailable, rarely at the office, fail to respond to calls, or fully neglect your employees or other followers, they will not listen to you effectively.

They're still going to work for you but only because they've got to. To get people to truly believe in you, to really understand how you can make them listen to you, then first you have to make sure you listen!

At the same time, you have to ensure that your employees or followers also have a high level of emotional intelligence. Show empathy and the ability to admit when you're wrong. Of course, if you're not at fault, you don't want to apologize outwardly but still prove you're willing to listen and reflect on the choices you make.

The focus, as a leader, is not simply on getting the job done. That's what the crowds are there for. As a leader, the job is to make sure people can do the job successfully because they're satisfied, their needs are met, and they're being looked after.

When you are knowledgeable, you can be a great boss and leader too. Always be willing to learn and understand something new, and make sure you keep up with the growth you are demonstrating to others. The more you can do that, the easier it will be for people to start trusting and believing in you and what you are trying to influence them.

5.4 Mind management for love and relationship with NLP

It's not just about improving the partnerships, either.

In the love we have for our family, NLP can help.

Practical NLP techniques work and give the confidence to use them more importantly. The fascinating thing is not only that it helps you not to get upset and disagree with anyone–it also allows them not to argue much with each other either, making home life much more enjoyable for everyone.

NLP can help you improve how you relate to others, how you listen, how you empathize with others, and how you respect other viewpoints. Of course, both of you will need to have the desire to strengthen your partnership and hopefully work together for a happier future, but if you are willing to work hard to develop and ensure improved communication with your partner, that in effect will lead to a healthier, happier relationship.

- Do you feel low concerning your relationship?
- Wonder what the future holds and whether you're going to make it through?

NLP will help you get back on track and whatever the result–NLP allows you to make decisions and feel great!

Chapter 6: How to Cope with Manipulations

The following section deals with how to cope with manipulation in different aspects of life. It tells about the tricks of how to cope with manipulations in various relationships such as marriages, with parents and children, with manipulative friends, in business, in leadership, with manipulative empathies, and with manipulative con artists.

6.1 How to cope with manipulations in love life

- **In Marriages**

Given the bonds and vows that bind couples together, marriage manipulation can be complicated to deal with compared to influencing other settings or situations. Nonetheless, there are ways of controlling the same thing so that someone isn't destined to become such a victim. Seduction was the first type of marital manipulation debated in the first chapter. A person who uses seduction as an instrument of coercion is likely to have addressed a combination of two of the traits. These are Machiavellian charisma and. Charisma is expected to be present as the person is going to bank a lot on his or her superficial charm to draw in their partners. It is the belief that their partners are irresistible that gives those seductive manipulators the strength they need to conduct their devious ploys. It's clear where the other feature, Machiavellianism, begins. The desire to lie and the ability to do so in a convincing way is a very critical prerequisite for seductive manipulation to succeed.

The silent treatment was the other manipulation of marital life. This is when someone distances himself emotionally from their partners when they are not happy with something. Again, it is possible to correlate this form of manipulation with some of the characteristics discussed. Narcissism and composure are the main ones to this. A person who acts in this way is not only infantile; he is also greedy and disrespectful to others ' feelings. These are A Narcissist's classic signs. The person's behavior regarding nonchalance is as if they don't matter how the relationship goes as long as you don't bend to their will. Indifference is how they get their partners to adapt, especially in situations where they know their spouses are involved in the relationships emotionally, financially, and physically.

The other form of marital coercion had been unexplained anger and tantrum-throwing. This form has all the psychopathy hallmarks to it. Such individuals capitalize on fear to get others to make their bidding. This is often characterized by different types and varying degrees of abuse in marriages, up to and including physical violence. The fear of such reactions, along with the desire for self-preservation, will force someone against their will to adhere to the other.

When you regularly observe these traits and manipulations in a marriage, appropriate action needs to be taken. It may be sufficient in many cases to get down and have an honest discussion with the perpetrator. In order to have better and more fruitful relationships, people need to have open conversations about their feelings. These conversations are especially useful where the victims are not aware of their actions. Others can indeed be exploited without meaning to. If the offended party does not resolve this problem, the manipulative habit will not only persist but will be intensified. Not all of these cases are salvageable. This is especially true with the final manipulative tactics of temper tantrums and abuse. It may be best to break up with the propagator in such situations, as there is no knowing what he might do next.

- **With Parents and Children**

There is a lot of manipulation going on in the family settings, as stated in the first chapter. Parents exploit their children all the time and vice versa, though the motives for doing so are often different for both classes. More often than not, parents ' manipulation of their children can be seen as positive. This is because, for the good of the goal, they are almost always finished.

In this context, however, malicious manipulations can occur within rare situations. For instance, there was a mother arrested for cocaine trafficking, using her son as an unsuspecting mule. He was consistently successful because the young boy never raised concern with the protection of the airport as a possible criminal and was therefore never subjected to extra scrutiny.

It is complicated to identify when our loved ones exploit us for their own benefit, as was the case in this example. This is because we are blinded by the love and trust we have for them so that we still live in denial of the apparent truth even when it is clear to all others to see the guile. When it comes to this issue, children are more fragile because they are still immature in every sense, emotionally, mentally, and physically. It is precisely for that reason that, when it comes to older people, especially their parents, they will almost always fall for manipulation.

It's a whole different thing when it comes to kids exploiting their parents. You may assume that this type of manipulation doesn't happen very often because children are often no wiser than their parents, but you're going to be wrong. Parents will fall solely out of love and a strong urge to protect them for the manipulations of their children. Parents need to be mindful that if they are continually falling for such manipulations, they may well be helping to endanger their children. If required, they must be able to exert tough love. A right way is like punishing if their children want to be disrespectful or deviant in a coercive manner. Such campaigns would dissuade children from similar abnormal potential behavior against their parents.

6.2 How to deal with social life manipulations

• With Manipulative Friends

Does your best friend manipulate you? You have that friend in your life you find it very difficult to say no to? Or do you have one that looks like you need your help every turn? You will learn to tell who of your friends are sincere and who of them will take you on a trip exploiting you for their own selfish gains. You need to be able to see which gifts your friends are, in fact, gestures of their goodwill and which ones are meant to soften you before you apply. You should learn to say no to some favors, particularly those that have strings attached to them, to be able to do this. By gaging your friend's reactions after you turn their gift down, you'll be able to know if what you turned down was a genuine gift or something else.

About the excellent snake, whenever they are in your business, you may want to pay more attention to what they say or do. The good snake is bound to try their tricks on almost anyone, and so if you spend a lot of time with them, there's a good chance they'll do it with you. Watch out for those people who like spreading rumors about them and bad mouthing others. If you are the object of the stories today, rest assured you'll be the focus tomorrow. Put a lot of consideration into how you react to their words, or how you let your perceptions affect the same. It would be helpful if you start showing disinterest or indifference to his or her stories after determining that your friend is a 'good snake.' This way, you'll slowly free yourself from their grip, and they'd leave you looking for new unsuspecting signs.

To compete with a deflector mate, you've got to have the same endurance as theirs when it comes to putting the point across. It means you will show the same passion, if not more, as they do when making the charges. Nonetheless, you must take precautions that you are very sure of them, lest you start accusing a truly innocent person. Once you are assured of your accusations, please stand up to your ground to make your claims and provide the necessary evidence where possible. Always take responsibility for something you weren't doing. And don't give in to their ploys under any conditions to alter the subject when they feel cornered. Instead, forge ahead and let them know very clearly that any attempt at deflection on their side is equivalent to a lost battle with you. By doing so, you'll be shielding yourself from deflection manipulation.

- **In Leadership**

Is your favorite leader real, or is he a wolf in the skin of the sheep? Does he live up to your expectations about his past pledges? These problems can be answered if we can avoid being exploited during campaign periods by such individuals. There are several forms of leadership, as you must have noted, and some manipulation is necessary and even encouraged in some situations of leadership. Nonetheless, the issue is the negative form of leadership exploitation and must be avoided at all costs. Some of the ways of doing so are illustrated below.

The best thing about dealing with iron fist rulers is to fight their ascension to power with all that you have. That may not, however, be enough to discourage such determined individuals. Considering their violent natures and very little respect for human life, laying low on this one may be advisable.

Away from dictator manipulation, there is a more common form of leadership manipulation. This is a manipulation of the political system. There is an explanation of why politics is widely considered a dirty game. It's because politicians are going to pull out all the stops, so they get what they want. Certain people, coercion is often the key to the game. Whether it's fellow politicians who have turned electorate rivals, aspiring leaders will say or do virtually anything if it guarantees them political arena survival. Their lies make it very difficult for people on their own behalf to make informed choices on their interests. It is for this reason that it is imperative to be able to tell apart from the few honorable lying manipulators.

One should develop a rational mind on the same campaign issue, too. Exaggeration is much used as a tool for manipulation, as mentioned. Taking a step back and taking the time with a clear mind to consider all the facts is all it takes to know when a politician is overbearing. More often than you might expect, a politician can exaggerate his or her dedication to service by vowing to fix other problems that may be out of their outlook in the first place. Where possible, when you detect such a lie, point out the discrepancies of such promises to protect others from being manipulated publicly. This is because personal refrain won't do any good to anyone, as if you could cast yourself their winning votes without publicity. If people here make these hyped promises, they feel lucky to have a politician sent from heaven. Little do these people know first of all that they are being manipulated?

Never believe any political propaganda when you are unable to check it. This is because their strong suits are not known for being either honest or decency. In the political game, mudslinging and slander is only the way of business. The victims are not only the targets of such lies, but they are also the ones who are fooled. This is because mass manipulation by misinformation consumes public opinion about various candidates and therefore has the power to deprive people of a cunning manipulator who is the otherwise perfect leader. Always try to find out the truth about such things. One way is to rely on credible news outlets that have been set up as such as opposed to listening to the numerous rumor-mongers that masquerade themselves as such.

As for the issue of luring campaign financiers, it is obvious how such manipulations can lead to public disservice. A perfect example of this is when the candidate has to pay back the financiers after a successful campaign. These paybacks are often at a great public expense. One might be expected to control the awarding of government tenders to their benefactors, for example. In many cases, these companies have a poor track record of performance or are obscenely inflating their rates, and as such, hiring them for anything will be tantamount to flushing public money down the drain.

To fix this includes tightening of campaign policies to prevent these manipulations. An excellent example of such tightening is to put a roof in the amounts that a single donor can give to a candidate in question. Another is by limiting individuals ' powers so that no one can make huge decisions that can enable them to fulfill their promises. These campaigns will take a long way in the future to prevent these manipulations at public expense.

6.3 How to treat business manipulations

This may be the most exploitative form of manipulation. Business manipulation means at least one person, the target, stands to lose money. It is specifically for this reason that everyone needs to be vigilant about the various manipulative tactics employed by business people. The next segment will look into how market manipulations can be resolved or prevented.

Concerning persuasive advertising, there are many things one can do to shield oneself from unscrupulous business people. The first, and most apparent, is relying on your own product or service experience. Always trust your opinions on items that you have had the opportunity to try, as opposed to trying new ones.

It's clear that this action plan has its shortcomings. First is that one can not have a preferred brand for everything he or she may want. The other drawback is that you may miss out on trying new items with the implied rigidity, which may actually represent real improvements from the ones you're used to. As such, when trying out new products, it is impossible to remain absolutely clear. The problem, therefore, remains the same. How to do so without falling prey to the techniques and manipulations of underhand business? There are several ways you could do that.

The first applies to the problem of vague or ambiguous product adverts. Just try to find out exactly what's included in the adverts. As far as the account is concerned, it is clear that the type of manipulation that targets only those who do not do their homework or are too forward when it comes to their wishes. If you want to buy a vehicle from a car dealer, for instance, don't get too enthusiastic about the particular model you want to buy. If you do, the car dealer will be given an arsenal to kill you during negotiations. This is because he would strive to upsell it much more than he would have done without the unnecessary excitement on your part, having known the vehicle that you are interested in.

On free samples, take them only when you have a genuine interest in buying the item. Remember that once you have received a free sample, you'll be more inclined to buy, regardless of whether you like it or not. This is because if you go up to a free sample stand, take your sample, then give negative feedback, let alone walk away; it will seem a little bit rude. You are more likely to reserve your feelings and make the purchase after taking a free sample, for fear of harming the sentiments of an apparent hard worker. So the trick is to refrain from taking any if you don't want to get yourself into an awkward position where you're forced to buy something against your will.

There's no foolproof plan to do so when it comes to preventing bribery in the company. That is because, with time and technology, the tactics evolve. The key is to exercise patience and listen to the advice that "When the price is too sweet, think twice." It might do you good to take a step back and consider, for example, why you have to buy the latest' if stocks last' hot stereo system when the one you've just worked perfectly. If you value your money or possessions, do your homework well and don't be an open book in your dealings for everyone to learn. A bit of a mystery will go a long way to protect you from the business world's bloodthirsty sharks?

6.4 How to Deal with Manipulative Empathy

Despite our apparent emotional susceptibility to empathy, it's quite hard to know when understanding affects us mentally, let alone controls it. Cultivating and exercising a robust emotional maturity and self-control is the best service you can do to yourself regarding this. Thus, although we cannot prevent empathy from perceiving our emotions, we will certainly prevent them from manipulating us as they wish.

6.5 How to deal with the Manipulative Con

There's a saying that' a sucker is born every minute and there's someone ready to take advantage of it for everybody.' While the accuracy of this statement may be disputed, one thing can not be discussed about it. This is the fact that so many people fall for other people's tricks as if they cannot think at all. But the sorrowful truth of the matter is that given the right timing and the right instruments, we are all suckers. A good con man will have a fully qualified accountant eating out of his hand on accounting matters, and the latter won't be the wiser to be taken for a ride.

When you let your guard down, make sure someone else doesn't hesitate to take advantage of you elsewhere. Understanding how they work is critical for shielding yourself from potential scammers. As already mentioned, these people of confidence play with the emotions of people and take advantage of your innermost desires by posing themselves as ideal vehicles for their fulfillment. Knowing this will formulate it much easier to identify and avoid the traps of an evil schemer who is out of your possessions to manipulate you.

The first thing you need to do when you are emotionally vulnerable is never to make crucial decisions or commitments. The problem here would, of course, be identifying your emotionally vulnerable moments. Rest assured that a seasoned con will see through all your pretensions, and you will become his intended target sooner rather than later.

It is essential to note at this stage that you are a potential target for trust artists, not just when you are emotionally weak. The opposite is also true and has been used in the past on several occasions with just as much if not more success. You're just as likely to make irrational decisions in moments of elation and euphoria as in moments of depression. If you don't want to be exploited or benefit from it, learn to recognize these times and then refrain from making important decisions.

The most attractive to the contras are moments of emotional confusion. This is because you are more likely to be receptive to its manipulative advances during these moments.

One way to avoid slipping into disadvantage tricks is through endurance drills. Never allow yourself to be rushed into any decisions against your will or better judgment because that's how the disadvantages work. A con will present his case in the most enticing manner while all the while hinting at the value of urgency for more income to succeed. This suggested urgency is meant to stop people from thinking about their idea twice and possibly second-guessing it, so this is precisely what you should do. Being patient is even more critical when you consider the deal is too good to be true because it probably is. You can expect a determined con to do his or her assignment concerning your most pressing needs and to approach you with precisely what you need at that particular time.

Conclusion

We have addressed all the things that are important to note throughout this book to avoid being manipulated, and to include constructive reinforcement in the way you communicate with others. It's not something that will be done immediately, but with more and more practice, you will realize that you have it all, whatever it takes to get the things you most want.

The biggest mistake some will make after learning these techniques is to use them to their benefit and take advantage of others instead of spreading the happiness and satisfaction gained from power. It's a lot easier to manipulate others negatively than to convince them positively. Often, convincing requires confidence-building.

Manipulation can be an installation of anxiety. While it may be easier to manipulate, it will eventually cause a lot more difficult things to clean up afterward!

Remember, this process starts with really understanding the personality of somebody. There are many common types of manipulators out there, and you may automatically be able to sense the character of nature in another human. You will also understand, equally, that there are secret characteristics that will not always appear at first.

Recalling recognizing that not all of an individual's manipulative behaviors indicate she is a malicious person. Getting manipulative parents or long-term relationships can rub off on our behavior, so sometimes we might say and do the things that aren't meant to be manipulative but can come off like that. When determining whether someone is manipulative or not, always look at intent.

However, don't forget that body language can play a significant role in how people are viewed. In others, you will begin to see convincing body language more often than before as soon as you become conscious of what this kind of body language looks like. Be sure you are aware of your body language so that others don't distort it.

Manipulation is generally away for a person to get the things they most want. We all have some basic needs and instincts which drive our actions. If we don't know how we get these things, then we can hurt someone. The more prepared we are with the skills required for positive influence, the easier it will be to fulfill our deepest wishes in a healthy manner that benefits others.

To keep your level of influence growing, remember that it begins with little moments of persuasion. Do not tell people what to do, inspire them from personal experiences and stories that others have heard. Don't try to trick anyone into the things they don't want to do. Be frank with incentive and effect so that they can make the decision properly for themselves.

Just make sure you're concentrating on your actions to make sure you don't go wrong. There is a certain level of confidence that goes along with being famous, too. If you're not careful, this trust will drive you too far ahead of others, and you may get lost in what you feel is best for everyone. The more you can reflect and ensure that you have the right intention, the easier it will be for you to encourage others genuinely.

While it may be challenging to do the right thing in times where you will also benefit most from what is most comfortable, remember to be empathetic towards others. Though it may be difficult, when you do so somewhat and satisfyingly, you will still eventually get the things you truly desire.

The Psychology of Persuasion - Part 2

Introduction

The Power of persuasion in today's world is of extraordinary and vital importance. Nearly every human experience involves and attempts to gain influence or persuade others to think our way. People are always trying to convince each other, regardless of age, gender, faith, or philosophical beliefs. We all want to be able to persuade and influence so that others listen to us, trust us, and follow us. A recent economists study found that a whopping 26 percent of gross domestic product was directly attributable to the marketplace's use of persuasion skills. Persuasion is the gas at the engine of our economy. Think about it-$ 2.3 trillion of our gross domestic product comes from the ability to believe and control. Large corporations seldom see their sales teams downsized. Sales managers are corporate assets and not liabilities. Even in the slowest economies, top-notch persuaders will always find employment.

Persuasion is a universal parable term. Persuasions may try and influence the values, attitudes, expectations, motives, or actions of an individual. Persuasion is the mechanism that leverages behaviors or convictions by appeals to logic and reason. In contrast, heuristic persuasion is the process through which attitudes or beliefs are leveraged through habit or emotional appeals. Persuasion is a literary tactic that authors use to influence the audience to view their ideas by reason and logic. Persuasion may simply use an argument to convince the readers, or can often force the readers to take some action. Simply put, it is an art of successful speech and writing in which authors, by reasoning, inducing feelings, and demonstrating their legitimacy, make their opinions right to the public.

Influence is who you are, and how the message can affect you as a person. It includes whether you are viewed as reliable and trustworthy; for example, Power enhances your ability to persuade and influence. This influence can be seen in a persuasive phase of people who possess the expertise, have authority, or use intimidation. Motivation is the ability to invite others to act according to the suggestions and ideas that you put forward. Persuasion is also a widely used tactic for seeking personal gain, such as running for votes, offering a sales pitch, or arguing in trials. Persuasion can also be defined as making use of one's personal or hierarchical Power to alter habits or attitudes of people. A woman with a business tries to persuade her colleagues. An example of persuading is when you argue strongly that your idea is right, and your argument convinces your employer to put your plan into action.

Power is the ability to convince, for good or evil. Think of all the people in your life who convinced you to go higher and achieve greatness. Persuasive people are keeping children off opioids, stopping conflicts, and improving lives. Convincing people, of course, also get children on drugs, stir up wars, and destroy lives. They want to focus on the Power of persuasion to better and strengthen ourselves, our friends and families, and our societies. The techniques of persuasion and manipulation are for the majority of us, not talents that we naturally possess. Naturally friendly, outgoing, and sometimes loud, there are the stereotypical persuaders. Evidence also reveals that some of the greatest persuaders are in fact, introverts. For many purposes, persuasion is necessary but perhaps the most important reason is that persuasion is a powerful vehicle of significant change, for good or for ill. In a free society, people are much more likely to be compelled to believe and do stuff than simply to be told what to think and what to do. Persuasion works best when people are both able to be convinced and unpersuaded. Some people simply take longer to be persuaded, and the persuaders present more of a challenge.

Nonetheless, the resistance to persuasion can be beneficial, especially if it triggers further thought and the resulting improvement in the persuader. After all, being persuaded of something doesn't mean that we have to get trapped with what we've become convinced. Ideally, resistance will lead the persuader either to find out more about his or her audience and why they resist, or to change his or her own beliefs following the audience's opinions. After all, the audience is sometimes closer to the truth (truth with a smaller case T) than the persuader. In a free society, free people are open to new ways of thinking and doing. Still, persuaders, who practice what they speak, who model the actions they want others to imitate, want to convince them to be ethically persuaded. In other words, they are looking for intelligent, decent, and highly credible and personable persuaders, with the audience's best interests at heart.

Persuasion is used by anyone who ever attempts to obtain something they want that requires the cooperation of any individual or group of people. Whether that is effective or ineffective, religious leaders use it (would anyone use the levy without a little persuasion?) Customers use it (negotiate salespeople rates and terms). Kids use it (they can get what they want). This is used by moms and dads (or else the above gets out of hand). It is used by politicians (without it, seek and gain public support). The salesmen use it (to sell products/services). Use it by friends (Always help someone move?). Life ultimately is all about convincing. Even growing up as a child, family, guardians, and friends have encouraged you to believe and to live the way you are now. So you also have to persuade your way through leadership or example to change or adjust your situation.

Chapter 1: What is Persuasion and influence?

A persuasion is a tricky form of art. When trying to persuade, it's easy to be unsuccessful but also surprisingly easy to overbear. Influence is who you are, and how the message will impact you as a person. This chapter will discuss the history of Persuasion, power of coercion, Persuasion in the modern age, congruent attitudes, and body language control, and tone of voice and consistency in behavior.

1.1 A short history of Persuasion:

Persuasion started with the Greeks, who emphasized Persuasion and eloquence as the highest standard for a successful politician; both proceedings were held in front of the house, and as they often do today, both the prosecution and the defense relied upon the speaker's persuasiveness. In any case, rhetoric has been the ability to find the available means of Persuasion. There are four reasons why one should learn the art of Persuasion:

- Truth and Justice are perfect; therefore, if a case loses, it is the fault of the speaker
- that is an excellent tool for teaching
- That a good rhetorician needs to know how to argue on both sides to
- Understand the whole problem and all the options, and
- That there is no better way to defend himself.

Persuasion is a public attraction. Ethos, logos, and pathos are all necessary appeals to persuade an audience. Rhetoric is the art of efficiently and persuasively using words. Rhetor is the message sent by the human.

Ethos

Ethos is an argument focused upon a speaker's character. A text motivated by principle or a form of Persuasion depends on the author's credibility. It refers to how the speaker or writer is trustworthy or truthful and how knowledgeable he or she is about a subject. If the audience is familiar with the speaker or writer, then their reputation here will be significant. Is she a Field Expert? Has she had relevant experience? If the speaker or writer is unfamiliar to the audience, then it is only through the text itself that she needs to establish ethos. Ethos is often conveyed through the message's tone and style, and through the way, the writer or speaker responds to differing views. Writers and speakers use ethos when connecting their argument to the set of aspects of their audience itself.

Logos

Logos is a rational appeal. By presenting reliable facts and statistics related to the topic at hand, using allusions, deductive reasoning, and referencing credible sources outside of the work itself, an author creates logos. While often associated with emotions, Greek for' suffering' or' experience' is more broadly an appeal that draws on the emotions, sympathies, interests, and imagination of the audience. The audience is encouraged to identify with the speaker or writer with an appeal for pathos-to feel or experience what the writer feels. As the sense of pathos means, what the rhetor experiences are what the viewer "suffers," in the realm of imagination.

Pathos

Pathos is an appeal to audience emotion. By including figurative languages such as metaphor, simile, and vivid imagery, an author develops pathos. Emotional anecdotes, the descriptive connotative language used to elicit compassion, and passionate interest in a subject may also be included. This refers to the consistency of the argument of the document; it's reasoning, and the validity of the supporting evidence. A simple progression of definitions backed up by reasonable and appropriate information should be followed by the audience.

Theories of Persuasion

Persuasion theories Understanding how people are convinced is very relevant for public-speaking conversation. Theories which help to explain why people are persuaded. While numerous theories help explain Persuasion, they do exist.

Attribution theory

Humans try to explain others ' actions by either dispositional attribution or situational attribution. Dispositional attribution, also called internal attribution, attempts to point to the characteristics, abilities, motives, or provisions of a person as a cause or explanation for their actions. A person who criticizes a president by claiming that the country lacks economic progress and safety because a dispositional interpretation is used by the president either lazy or deficient in economic intelligence. Situational attribution, often referred to as external attribution, tends to point to the context surrounding the individual and factors surrounding him, especially things that are entirely beyond his control. A citizen claiming a lack of economic progress is not the president's fault, but rather the fact that he inherited the previous president's weak economy is situational attribution. A fundamental error in attribution occurs when people incorrectly attribute either failure or success to internal factors and ignores any external factors. In general, when attempting to justify or understand a person's actions, people tend to make dispositional attributions more often than situational attributions. This happens when we're far more individually focused because we don't know much about their situation or context. We tend to explain positive behaviors and achievements with dispositional attribution when trying to persuade others to like another person or us but our negative actions and shortcomings with situational attributions.

Behavior change theories

The theory of expected actions is the primary theory of behavioral change. It has meta-analysis help that shows that it can predict around 30% of behavior. Theories but internal validity priorities by nature, over external validity. They are coherent, making a story easy and re-appropriate. On the other hand, they can correlate more poorly with the facts and dynamics of experience than a simple explanation by their efficacy of behavior change strategies (techniques). Behavioral psychologists have identified these behavior change strategies. A mutually exclusive, comprehensive (MECE) translation of this taxonomy in decreasing order of effectiveness is:

- Positive and negative effects
- Offering, removing incentives
- Offering, eliminating threats and punishments
- Distraction
- Changing exposure to behavioral signs (triggers)
- Prompts, cues,

- The setting of goals,

Cognitive dissonance theory

This theory theorized that human beings always strive for mental consistency. Their cognition (thought, perception, or attitude) may be in agreement, incompatible, or discord with one another. Their reasoning can also be compatible with or disagree with their behaviors. This gives us a sense of incompleteness and discomfort when we detect conflicting cognition or dissonance. A person who is addicted to smoking cigarettes, for example, but also suspects it might be detrimental to his health, suffers from cognitive dissonance.

Once our consciousness is in agreement with itself, we are driven to reduce this dissonance. We strive for consistency in mentality. There are four main ways to reduce or eliminate our inconsistency:

- To change our minds about one of the facets of cognition
- Reducing the importance of cognition
- Increasing the overlap between the two
- And to re-evaluate the cost, reward ratio.

Reviewing the smoker's example, either he can quit smoking, minimize the value of his health, reassure himself that he is not at risk, or that smoking's benefit is worth the cost of his health.

Cognitive dissonance is essential when it involves rivalry and a sense of self. The most famous example of how to use cognitive dissonance for an experiment of Persuasion In which participants were asked for an hour to complete a very slow mission. Some were paid $20 while others were paid $1 and told to inform the next waiting participants that the experiment was fun and exciting afterward. Those paying \$1 were far more likely to convince the following participants that the investigation was entertaining than those earning \$20. This is because \$20 is justification enough to take part in an hour-long tedious mission, so there is no dissonance. Those who won \$1 felt tremendous dissonance, so they had to genuinely reassure themselves that the role was enjoyable to avoid taking advantage of the feeling and thus their dissonance.

Elaboration likelihood model

Traditionally, the Persuasion model of creation probability has been correlated with two paths.

Central route: whereby a person considers information provided to them based on its pros and cons and how well it suits their principles Peripheral route: Change is driven by how appealing the medium of communication is and bypassing the mechanism of deliberation.

The Elaboration probability model (ELM) is forming a new facet of route theory. This claims that the probability of effective Persuasion depends on how efficient the communication is in remembering a related mental image, which is the likelihood of elaboration. So if the contact goal is personally relevant, this increases the probability of the intended outcome being conveyed and would be more convincing if it were through the middle path. Communication that doesn't need careful thinking would be better suited to the peripheral road.

Functional theories

In different situations, functional theorists attempt to understand the divergent attitudes individuals have towards people, objects or issues. There are four principal useful attitudes: Adjustment function: An individual's primary motivation is to increase positive external rewards and minimize costs. Opinions tend to steer reward actions and away from punishment. Ego Defensive function: The mechanism by which a person protects their ego from being harmed or damaged by their negative impulses.

Value-expressive: When a person derives gratification from presenting a picture of himself that is in line with his self-concept and the values with which he wishes to be associated.

Role of knowledge: The need to get a sense of understanding and power over one's existence. Hence, the attitudes of a person serve to help set standards and rules that regulate his or her knowledge of being.

If communication addresses an underlying function, the degree of persuasiveness determines how people change their attitude after deciding that another approach will serve the purpose more effectively.

Inoculation Theory

A vaccine introduces a weak form of a virus that can be easily defeated to prepare the immune system if a stronger type of the same infection is to be combated. The inoculation theory suggests in much the same way that a particular party will implement a weak version of an argument that is easily overcome to make the audience likely to ignore a stronger, full-fledged form of that argument from an opponent's party.

This often occurs in negative advertising and competitive advertisements — both for goods and for political reasons. An example would be a product maker showing an ad that refutes a specific claim made about the product of a competitor so that when the audience sees an ad for that rival company, they immediately deny the demands of the product.

Narrative transportation theory

Narrative theory of transport implies that when people lose themselves in a tale, their perceptions and expectations shift to represent that story. The mental state of narrative transportation may clarify the persuasive impact of stories on people who, when certain contextual and personal preconditions are met, may perceive narrative transportation as Green and Brock postulate for the model of transportation imaging. Tale transportation happens when the reader of the story feels a sense of entering a world evoked by the tale because of empathy for the protagonists of the story and the plot's imagination.

Social judgment theory

The theory of social judgment Suggests that when people come up with an idea or any kind of convincing suggestion, their natural reaction is to seek a way to subconsciously organize the information and react to it immediately. We evaluate and equate the knowledge with the attitude we already have, which is called the initial position or anchor point.

When attempting to sort out incoming persuasive information, an audience determines whether it lands in its latitude of acceptance, the scope of non-commitment or indifference, or the latitude of refusal. Those latitudes vary in size from topic to topic. The "ego-implication" usually plays one of the most critical roles in deciding the scale of these latitudes. When a question is closely related to how we define and perceive ourselves, or when dealing with anything that we care passionately about, our acceptance and non-commitment latitudes are likely to be much smaller, and our rejection attitude much larger. The anchor point of an individual is known as the center of his acceptance latitude, the location which is most appropriate to him.

A public is likely to misinterpret incoming information to fit into its particular latitudes. If something falls within the acceptability latitude, the subject tends to assimilate the information and consider it closer to its point of an anchor than it is. Conversely, if something falls within the latitude of rejection, the subject tends to contrast the information and convince himself that the data is farther away than it is from his anchor point.

It is essential to first know the average latitudes of approval, non-commitment, and rejection of your audience while trying to persuade a specific target or an entire audience. If the goal is to shift the anchor point of the audience, it is optimal to use convincing information that lands near the boundary of the latitude of acceptance. Repeatedly suggesting ideas at the fringe of acceptance latitude makes people adjust their anchor points gradually while suggesting ideas in the scope of rejection or even the latitude of non-commitment does not change the anchor point of the audience.

1.2 What is Persuasion in the modern age?

In the modern era, Persuasion in the form of advertising is most evident. Persuasion can be analyzed preliminarily by distinguishing communication (as the cause or stimulus) from the associated changes in attitudes (as the effector response. In today's world, Persuasion is of intense and critical importance. Nearly every human experience involves an attempt to gain influence or convince others to think our way. People are always trying to convince each other, regardless of age, gender, faith, or philosophical beliefs. They all want to be able to convince and motivate so that others listen to us, believe us, and obey us. A recent economists study found that a whopping 26 percent of gross domestic product was directly attributable to the marketplace's use of persuasion skills. Persuasion is the gas at the heart of our economy. Think of it— $2.3 trillion of our gross domestic product comes from Persuasion skills and power. Large corporations seldom see their sales teams downsized. Sales managers are corporate assets and not liabilities. Even in the slowest economies, top-notch persuaders will always find employment. Power is the ability to convince, for good or evil. Think of all the people in your life who inspired you to go higher and achieve greatness. Persuasive people are keeping children off opioids, stopping conflicts, and improving lives. Naturally, manipulative people are also getting children on drugs, stirring up wars, and destroying lives. We want to reflect on Persuasion's power to improve and strengthen ourselves, our friends, families, and our communities. But let's face it: Most of us aren't born persuaders. The arts of Persuasion and power for the majority of us are not talents we naturally possess. Naturally polite, confident, and sometimes rude, there are the stereotypical persuaders. Research also reveals that some of the strongest persuaders are, in fact, introverts.

The notion of becoming a polished persuader means being strong, manipulative, or pushy for many. An inference like that is dead wrong. Tactics like these may have short-term effects, but Maximum Impact is about long-term results. Durable power is not derived from calculated tricks, malicious manipulation, or intimidation. Instead, the correct application of the latest techniques of Persuasion will allow you to influence with the utmost integrity. Naturally and instinctively, people will trust you, believe you, and want you to convince them. In short, what you want them to do will they want to do. It is a common misconception that only individuals involved in roles of sales, marketing, or leadership need to know the Persuasion Rules. That just isn't real! Such skills can be used by sales staff, business managers, parents, negotiators, attorneys, coaches, talkers, marketers, and doctors alike. Everybody wants persuasive skills, no matter how busy they are. What people don't realize is that everybody uses Persuasion methods and strategies every day. People are always researching each other, trying to figure out how they can get somebody to do what they want. Mastering communication and understanding human nature are essential lessons of life if we are to persuade people and influence them effectively. Unless we can interact with other human beings, we cannot get anywhere in life. The success we achieve is through our relations with others. Nobody is autonomous. Through the support and help of the people around us, everything of any importance we achieve in life is accomplished. We are interconnected as a society, and the ability to make those connections is essential to our progress.

Persuasion is the most common technique used in literature. We consider it not only in literature but also in political speeches, conferences, courtrooms, and advertising. Writers express their feelings and thoughts by persuasive writing, emotionally and rationally appealing to the audience. Hence, winning over readers or viewers is a valuable strategy. It also helps students to discover specific reasons in support of their opinions and provides them with an opportunity to explore evidence similar to their beliefs. Students can understand the nature of persuasive work when gaining an understanding of how writing can alter and affect their thoughts and actions. An example of Persuasion is when you argue strongly that your proposal is right, and your argument convinces your employer to bring your strategy into action.

1.3 The Power of influence

Influence is the power to have a significant effect on someone or something. If someone influences someone else, they are changing a person or thing in an indirect but essential way. Influence as a skill refers to the ability to make a positive impact on others, to convince them or to encourage them to gain support. You are convincing and interacting with the Influence of competency, and you can create buy-in from critical people. Take this example: A managing director who headed a Manhattan-based company decided to move the corporation to 1,000 miles away from a small city. He hoped to save money because of tax advantages and cheaper labor. He had also grown up there and never felt at ease in Manhattan. But it resulted in a wave of people leaving after he made the change.

They didn't want to go into that little town. He lost the IT workers primarily to men. A lot of critical, unwritten knowledge went with them about how IT worked at that organization. The company ended up having to hire former employees to get crucial information for a large consulting fee. The CEO's lack of Influence Competency skills cost his business a lot of money and lost revenue. Influence has a strong positive impact on any executive's success. This may be especially true for members who report to them, for example, in many different groups. Note, leadership is the art of getting other people to get work done well. And persuasion is the most powerful form of doing that. In the same way, when you work with a division over which you have no direct authority, power is also important, because their work is vital for your own success. You can't order them to do whatever you want; you have to convince or encourage them to do their best towards the clear goal you have set. We're all leaders to the degree that each of us has a personal sphere of Influence. The visionary leader–who articulates a deeply felt dream that resonates with and motivates many–reveals one clear use of power when it comes to leadership styles. Yet acting as a coach and mentor, another leadership style (and another skill), opens the way for a personal connection that can be a highway for influencing the person itself.

Two other types of leadership— the consensus-seeker and the affiliate leader who sees the value of having a good time together — build the kind of positive relationships that allow them to exert Influence during their ordinary interaction. Through the use of Influence, all these styles have a positive impact on the emotional climate. One essential leadership skill is the ability to influence. Influencing involves having an impact on other people's behaviors, beliefs, views, and choices. Power or control should not be confused with Influence. It is not a matter of exploiting others to get your way. It is about noticing what motivates employee engagement and making use of that knowledge to leverage performance and positive results. The ability of a leader to influence others is based on trust; our power is expanding in proportion to the amount of trust that exists in a relationship. Let's look at how leaders can create confidence efficiently, and through their leverage with others.

There are four primary causes. Impact forms include negative, neutral, constructive, and life-changing.

Negative Influence

The first type is negative, and the most damaging Influence. People with this kind of control tend to concentrate on their authority, power, or title. Often they are egocentric and prideful. These are the leaders who have difficulty getting people to follow them, respect them, or listen to them. Their effect leaves the affected team or company in a negative or wrong way, mainly as a result of the negative Influence the team creates through the poor results. Do whatever you can to prevent influences of this type.

Neutral Influence

This form of Influence's actions and attitude appear to neither attach nor subtract from what those around do. If a person with this type of Influence were within a group of people, they would not need to do anything that would make them stand out or be seen as a leader. We don't lead, support, or take responsibility proactively. These are the people with the position or title but who do not maximize that position in a way that advances the team or organization. The people (staff) often have to lead and inspire themselves to produce results, as the leader won't encourage them to do so. Note, these first two forms of power you'll want to stop. Let's see what kind of Influence you should be striving to get.

Positive Influence

A leader with this form of power adds meaning, and because of the actions and attitude of this person, it makes the people you come into contact with better off. They are actively leading, building relationships with others, and are present, all in attempts to inspire, coach, and lead people to better outcomes. They want to have a positive impact on the lives of those they are leading, helping them succeed in all areas of their lives. Positive Influence requires a high degree of intentionality, time, and commitment, but the outcome will be that everyone will be happier and do better because you are the leader. Influence transforming life This is the highest and most important form of Influence. Few people have this level of Influence or attain it. To gain life-changing power, it takes years or decades to lead well and with a positive effect. Several examples of influencers who change lives include Jesus Christ, Mother Teresa, Oprah Winfrey, John C. Maxwell, and Abraham Lincoln.

Life-changing Influence

Life-changing effect is about having an impact on someone if their life is changed forever as a result of what you have done and said. Many of your implications, in this way, stay influenced by positivity even after you have left the team or organization. This involves spending all of your time and energy in supporting and helping others succeed and become successful in life and at work. It's about setting out your wishes and adding value to others. The sacrifice is worth the return because you will have people who are loyal and dedicated and willing to do anything for you.

1.4 Congruent Attitudes

This is a type of change of attitude in which the current attitude changes in the same direction. The current attitude towards the target is further strengthened-e.g. a positive attitude becomes more positive, and a negative attitude becomes more negative.

For instance, a person's attitude toward gym exercises is positive. When he gets to know more about the physical benefits of gym workouts and spend more time engaging in gym exercises-this sort of the change in attitude is called a congruent shift in attitude. A person likewise has a negative attitude toward waking until late at night. If he gets to know more about the health complications of waking until late at night, his negative attitude towards waking late at night becomes more negative–it's a congruent change of attitude. A position is a negative or positive assessment of an item. It expresses the love or dislike of an individual toward an object, or to favor or disadvantage an object. A vegetarian person, for example, has a negative attitude to beef consumption and avoids eating beef. One can change the attitude towards an object from time to time. For example, if a vegetarian who has a negative attitude towards beef consumption discovers that beef is rich in vitamins which are essential for human health, he may develop a positive attitude towards beef consumption and begin to include meat in his daily diet. Occasionally, it is intended to influence or alter a group of people's current attitudes toward an object; it can be achieved using various techniques such as commercials, speeches, seminars, etc. For example, television ads are designed to influence or alter people's attitudes toward a product favorably to increase product selling. Persuasion is also a technique for shaping or changing people's attitudes.

1.5 Control Body Language and Voice Tone

Experts say you should teach yourself to control it by becoming aware of your body language, and even actively use it to make your speech "Learn to use body language by reading a body language dictionary is like trying to speak French by reading a French dictionary," writes Driver. Your actions seem robotic; your body language skills seem disconnected from one another." Instead of trying to alter or mask your natural body language, Drivers suggests striving to refine and clarify it, so that it reinforces rather than distracts from the message you're trying to convey. 16 Ways to control Body Language Here are 16 ways to understand and improve your own body language.

1. Be Aware

The first step to body language improvement is awareness. Start to pay attention to everything you do, and when you do it. The other day, I noticed I play with my earring when talking to certain people or about certain topics; with that realization I can better understand why I do it and what it means. Awareness is half the battle.

2. Study Others

Look at other people — especially people you admire. How do they hold themselves? What can you learn from them?

3. Mirror the Other Person

If you are sitting or standing opposite somebody, mirror their body positions, match their tone, and carry the same pace of conversation. Don't do it in an obvious or unnatural fashion. Even subtle mirroring can create a synergy and connection, and after a while, you'll both be doing it naturally — you won't even know who is following who.

4. Be Aware of How You Cross Your Arms and Legs

Many people find crossing arms or legs comfortable, so it's no use to say you can't do it. If you want to cross your legs, that's okay; just be aware of the direction your cross them in, and make sure you cross towards your conversation partner. Beware: crossing your legs in a "figure four" fashion with your ankle resting on your knee can be seen as being stubborn or arrogant. Also, be aware of other ways of creating crosses with your body; women often grab their opposite shoulder or elbow, or people hold a drink on the table using the opposite hand: these are signs of a lack of confidence or closing your body (and mind) to the conversation.

5. Make Eye Contact

Eyes are windows to the soul, and what you do with them communicates a lot. Be sensitive to cultures that eschew eye contact with elders or strangers; otherwise, don't be afraid to look somebody in the eye. Not only will you say a lot by doing so, but you might also learn a lot.

6. Relax Your Shoulders

Holding your shoulders by your ears is a sign of tension, and stands to put your conversation partner on edge as well.

7. Don't Slouch

Although sitting ram-rod straight might be a forced exaggeration, make sure you're not slouching. Your back — and social life — will benefit.

8. Face Your Conversation Partner

Similar to crossing arms and legs, not facing your conversation partner is a sign of distraction or disinterest. You'll increase engagement by facing your partner.

9. Lean In

Have you ever had a conversation that you're both enthusiastic about? You'll probably notice you both are lively and leaning in towards each other.

10. Mind Your Fidgeting

I'm a sucker for playing with my drink, or straw, an earring, or a bottle cap — with what I affectionately refer to as a "tactile fixation." But it can be a sign of nervousness and, at the very least, a distraction for others. Also watch out for touching your face or running your hands through your hair.

11. Don't Tilt Your Head (Too Much)

Although a slight tilt of your head can indicate interest, too much of a head tilt (women are the main culprits for this) indicates submissiveness.

12. Don't End Sentences with Upswings

Although intonation isn't quite a body language, it warrants mentioning since it's part of the subconscious messages we communicate. Ending your sentences like questions indicates a lack of confidence in what you're saying, which does nothing to instill others' confidence in you.

13. Go for a Firm or Matching Handshake

Don't squeeze the life out of your new acquaintance, but a nice firm handshake feels good. I tend to try to match my acquaintance's handshake (like mirroring) — except for wet fishes. I just can't do it.

14. Know Where Your Hands Are

Holding your arms behind your back with your hands clasped is a sign of confidence. (It also provides you with something for your hands to do if you fidget! This is great for public speaking. Conversely, holding your hands in your pockets might be comfortable, but can also indicate boredom or over-confidence.

15. Sit in an Engaging Position

Unless your star-crossed lovers gazing into one another's eyes, sitting directly opposite somebody indicates confrontation. It's even worse with a table or desk in between you, which creates a barrier. Instead, try to sit at a 45 degree angle. This provides comfort, space, and still allows you to mirror and engage.

16. Relax

Now that you're probably hyper-aware of everything you do and don't do take a deep breath and relax. Adjusting your body language might feel unnatural at first, so don't force it too much. With a dose of awareness and applying these techniques gently over time, you'll communicate everything you want to with your words as well as your body.

Control voice tone:

As we speak to each other, we express more than just the words that we use. We watch the body language of each other and listen to the tone of voice of the people. If you are having a casual, happy conversation with someone, talk in a friendly tone is essential. To do so, adjust your body language and speech style. Soon you can sound as lovely as you can be.

Breathe from your diaphragm to control your voice: Making your voice tone friendlier requires you to be aware of how fast you are speaking, and how high and low your voice is getting for better control using deep breaths from your abdomen. To check that you breathe from your diaphragm (the muscle that sits right under your lungs), watch yourself in the mirror while breathing in. You take shallow breaths without using your diaphragm if your shoulders and chest rise. Practice using your diaphragm by placing your hand on your abdomen while you breathe in and pushing it outwards.

Vary your vocal pitch: Do not speak with a monotonous voice. Instead, make your voice as you speak up high and low.

Stressing essential words with a higher tone in your sentence reassures listeners while lower pitches will inject harmony into your conversation. Start questions on a higher pitch and lower pitch comments. If you end top pitch statements, you'll sound like you don't believe what you've just said. The best way to maintain a friendly tone is to have varied pitches while you're talking. You don't want to have a totally high-pitched conversation, because people might think you've just inhaled a balloon of helium. However, a completely low-pitched conversation might make your listener think you are uninterested in chatting with them. Speak slowly to keep people engaged: If you talk too quickly, you just sound like you want your conversation to be over and done. Speak slowly, instead, so that your listener can hear every word you say. This is going to tell them that you want to talk to them there. You don't have to take 30 seconds to get every word out. Be aware of your speed, and of course, you're going to slow down. Add a few pauses to allow your listener to keep up. Use a softer voice to avoid sounding aggressive: There is nothing worse than feeling like someone is yelling at you. Keep your voice to the point that lets people hear you without crying out to them.

Breathing out of your diaphragm will help with this problem. Those regulated breaths allow everyone to hear you without having you working too hard to get the sound out. Each time you struggle to make yourself heard, you'll likely end up yelling, which won't sound pleasant.

1.6 Behavioral Consistency

Behavioral consistency refers to the tendency of people to behave in a way that fits previous actions or behaviors. Behavioral consistency is a heuristic assumption to which we resort to facilitate decision-making: it is easier to make one decision and to remain consistent with it than building a new decision whenever a problem arises. From an evolutionary point of view, behavioral continuity often serves us well: erratic people are less likely to be accepted and to succeed in a social environment, among others. People will not only go out of their way to behave consistently, but they will also have a definite feeling of being consistent with their decisions, even when they face evidence that their choices were wrong. Behavioral consistency acts at both the individual and the social level "Once we make a choice or take a stand, we will encounter personal and interpersonal pressures to behave consistently with that commitment. These pressures will cause us to respond in ways that justify our earlier decision. "Let's say you're resolving to go to the gym at 6:00 a.m. three times a week. Once that decision is made, you'll feel compelled to stick with it. This is the nature of people— the desire to keep a promise made to themselves. On the social level, this motivation will be even stronger— that is, if the pledge is public and includes others: if you and a partner agree to meet in the morning at the gym, you'll feel more committed to your commitment and more likely to follow through. While inconsistency with ourselves can lead to some culpability, inconsistency with others leads to interpersonal risk. Inconsistency is viewed as an unwelcome characteristic and is associated with irrationality, deception, and even incompetence; it can cause frustration, rage, and confusion reactions. These risks create tremendous pressure on society to remain consistent. Thus, people will endeavor to make sure their behavior matches past decisions to avoid undue stress. Because of these personal and social pressures, if you're making people commit to something, they're likely to try to keep going. The commitment needn't be a big one. It's often, in reality, a small decision. It could have been an off-hand, seemingly inconsequential remark on a bottle of New Year's Eve champagne, in the case of our fitness resolution. And, in my parents' fact, this was a dismissive response to a dog's pleas. My father would answer, "Perhaps when you're older," in hopes I'd forget. I further nagged, "How much older? "And finally my mother caved and said, "Maybe when you're ten years old. "Every year, I counted the remaining years until a dog owed me. They kept their word real and, much to their chagrin; I was the proud owner of a spaniel named Toby when I turned ten years old. He lived an astonishing 11 years. And my parents loved him in a hilarious (but predictable) turn of events.

Chapter 2: Laws of Persuasion

After discussing the history of persuasion, it is now time to discuss the laws and secrets method of persuasion. This chapter will look at the six laws of persuasion that can help you understand the psychology of persuasion better.

2.1 Laws of Persuasion

Persuasion is the ability through specific strategies to influence thoughts and actions. To master that skill, some basic principles, called the Laws of Persuasion, must be understood. Six laws make up the Persuasion Laws that explain how most people respond to some circumstances. The Psychology of Persuasion, in which the powerful persuasion techniques are explored. Some psychological research shows that humans are quite consistent in terms of behavior in response to certain stimuli, such as advertising. This is why companies spend so much money on advertising, and why customers respond by buying the products and services, they advertise to most advertisements and commercials. An understanding of the Laws of Persuasion helps you to monitor how others unduly influence you, and how you can use the laws to your advantage during negotiation.

People face countless decisions every day, and the laws work because they provide shortcuts for many of those decisions to be made. Some of the best negotiating masters of the art of persuasion are highly successful salespeople who do their best not only to make the sale but also to meet the needs of their buyers. Our fundamental goal as project managers is to meet the needs of stakeholders, so these Laws of Persuasion give us another tool that we can use to increase our influence over others as we guide the project towards success.

Six Laws of Persuasion are:

- Law of Reciprocity
- Law of Commitment and Consistency
- Law of Liking
- Law of Scarcity
- Law of Authority
- Law of Social Proof

1. Law of Reciprocity

Generally speaking, people try to repay what others have got. If somebody gives you something you want, then you are going to want to reciprocate because you feel obliged now. For example, the address labels you receive from various non-profit groups requesting charitable donations in the mail— even though they are a minor, unsolicited "gift," sending them out has significantly increased contributions to non-profits because people feel compelled to "return the favor." In projects, there are always opportunities to use the Law of Reciprocity. If you have accepted a team member's demand for the timing of his or her work on a task, you can use reciprocity to receive concession from him or her when you need something next. When negotiating procurement with vendors, the use of restricted disclosure or apology for the real reason of a negotiating stance, such as "this is all the money we have," may cause the other party to make a concession. Concessions generally follow that "tit-for-tat" rule (the better, of course, the lower the "value" of your permit). The reciprocity rule is essential because a sense of obligation can be overpowering and instill in us. Generally, when offered a free service or gift, we have a dislike for people who neglect to return a favor or provide payment. Reciprocation is thus a widely held concept. This societal standard makes reciprocity a compelling, persuasive technique, as it can lead to unequal exchanges and can even apply to uninvited first favor. Because of its use as a powerful, persuasive technique, reciprocity refers to the marketing sector. The "free samples" marketing tactic demonstrates the reciprocity rule because of the sense of obligation that the state creates. That sense of responsibility stems from the desire to repay the marketer for a "free sample" gift.

2. Law of Commitment and Consistency

Consistency is an essential aspect of persuasion because of it:

- Culture is highly valued,
- Results in a positive approach to everyday life and
- Offers a convenient shortcut through the complex nature of modern existence.

It is necessary to have coherence (or at least the appearance of) thoughts, feelings, and actions. Once a stance is taken, people tend to stick with it and behave in ways that justify the position, even if it is incorrect. Commitment to an (although small) decision, place, or cause is usually easier to increase than abandon. That's why salespeople try to get customers to agree with them multiple times; after repeatedly saying "yes," it's nearly impossible to say "no" when it's time for the closing or direct sale request. An application of this law would be to ask a series of questions to confirm the acceptance of each particular component of a system before requesting approval of the entire system. In How to Win Friends and Influence People, Dale

Carnegie called this, "Get the other person saying' yes, yes' right away." This happens when one party asks the other side to make several "small" decisions, which lead to only one obvious conclusion: accept the general concession. Examples of this can also be seen in the use of low-balling tactics, in which deliberate, last-minute additions to what was originally a low price are made. Here the selfish goal is to get you to "invest" in a commodity that you initially thought cost less. Consistency enables us to make decisions and process the information more effectively. The concept of consistency states that someone who commits to something is more likely to honor that commitment, orally, or in writing. This is particularly true for written promises, as they become more tangible psychologically and can generate hard evidence. Someone who commits to a role appears to act upon that commitment. Commitment is an effective persuasive technique, because once you get someone to invest, they are more likely to engage in self-persuasion, giving reasons and justifications for supporting their commitment to avoid dissonance, to themselves and others. Another reason is that children are made to repeat the Pledge of Allegiance every morning and why advertisers are making you close popups by saying, "I will sign up later" or "No thanks, I prefer not to make money.

3. Law of Liking

The adage of "attracting opposites" does not hold when shaping and persuading people. If you like someone or think they're "just like you," you're more likely to want to satisfy them. Successful salespeople are working hard to establish relationships, to prove how similar they are to you. They explore your background and note their similarities. They're people that you know; your friends sometimes. Think of the in-home sales parties to which you may have been invited, where your neighbors provide the testimonials for the product, and you don't want to offend them by not purchasing something. The lesson from, and from the implementation of, the Law of Liking in sales is the importance of reporting. If you can establish a relationship with your team or other stakeholders, you can create the commonality or connection between you and increase your chance to influence their decisions. If you need to convince the team to work harder, you can use the Law of Liking; when team members feel that you are also taking on more work, and you appreciate their "pressure," then they may be more willing to go the extra mile. In sales, we also see this in the "good cop, bad cop" tactic. The "bad cop" obviously supports your aims while the "good cop" appears to support your stance. You will, of course, tend to identify with the "good cop," sometimes agreeing with their demands and priorities rather than your own. People are saying "yes" to those people they like. Two major factors contribute to a general resemblance. The first is the physical appeal. Physically attractive individuals seem more convincing. We get what they want, and can easily change the attitudes of others. This attractiveness has been shown to send favorable messages/impressions of other traits a person may have, such as talent, kindness, and intelligence; The second factor is a similitude. We are more easily convinced by people that we see as being similar to ourselves.

4. Law of Scarcity

If there is a limited supply of an object, and only a few are left, then it must be excellent or standard, as implied by the scarcity rule. If something you want becomes "the last available one," you tend to feel like you need to act right away, or you might miss it out. The limited supply must, after all, mean that others are buying it, and delaying might mean that you won't be able to get it anytime soon or maybe never again. There are always constraints on time, money, and people in projects. The Scarcity Law tells us that the less of something there is, the more it may be desired. You can use the limitations to manipulate stakeholders to set scope or task goals or negotiate commitment to a higher allocation of time for a resource to the project.

Scarcity may play an essential role in the persuasion process. When something has a restricted supply, it is more important than people give. "People want more of what they can't have," If scarcity is an issue, the context matters. That means deficiency "works" better within specific contexts. To order to get people to assume that something is scarcer, advertisers explain what does no other product does about that particular product. Marketers also get people to believe that something is scarce by asking them what they're going to lose, not what they're going to gain — using phrases like, "You're going to lose \$5," rather than, "Save \$5." There are two main reasons why the theory of scarcity works:

- If things are hard to get, they're typically more expensive so that they can appear higher quality.
- We may lose the chance to acquire them as items become less available.

When that happens, we assign more value to the scarce item or service simply because it's more challenging to acquire.

That principle is that we all want things beyond our reach. If we see that something is readily available, then we don't want it as much as something very unusual.

5. Law of Authority

When using celebrity endorsements or "expert" testimonies, advertisers count on the law of authority. If you admire people promoting a product or service, you may think, "If it's good enough for them, then it's good enough for me." Moreover, if you're using it, you may become more like these "heroes" that look better, wealthier, and more famous. Use the authority law to establish your credentials or credibility in the negotiation process early on. To gain credibility, relate your position to known, respected sources when setting your schedule or explaining how or why decisions have been made. We tend to believe that it must be real if an expert says anything. People like listening to those who are knowledgeable and trustworthy, so if you can be these two things, you're already on your way to making people believe and listen to you.

A "teacher" and a "learner" were placed in two distinct rooms in the Milgram study. The "learner" was connected to an electrical brace that was able to administer a shock. A boss, dressed in the coat of a white scientist, instructed the "teacher" to put questions to the learner and punish him when he got a question wrong. The study supervisor had asked the teacher to deliver an electric shock from a panel under the control of the teacher. The instructor had to move up the voltage to the next notch after delivery. The energy ascended to 450 volts. The catch to this experiment was that the teacher did not know that the learner was an actor who invented the sounds of pain he felt and was not hurt. The test was being performed to see how obedient to authority we are. "When an authority tells ordinary people that it is their job to harm, how much suffering will each subject be willing to inflict on an entirely innocent another person if the instructions come' from above?'" The results of this study show that most teachers were willing to give as much pain as they could. The conclusion was that people are eager to bring pain upon others when some figure of authority directs them to do so.

6. Law of Social Proof

As humans, we are influenced by others around us; we want to do what all the rest are. Individuals frequently base their actions and beliefs on what others are doing around them, how others are behaving, or what others think. "Crowd power" is beneficial. We all want to know what those around us are doing. We are so concerned with what other people are doing and how others are behaving that we then seek to be like others. In a phone–a–thon, the host says something like, "Operators are waiting, please call now." The only context you have from that statement is that the operators are waiting and not busy. Instead, the host might say: "If the operators are busy, please call again." This is the social proofing technique. It sounds like the lines are busy, and other people are calling, just by changing three words, so it has to be a worthwhile organization.

Social proof is most effective when people are unsure or when a situation has similarities. When multiple possibilities create choices we must make in uncertain or ambiguous situations; people are likely to conform to what others do. In circumstances that pose a decision, we get more affected by the people around us. The other useful social proofing case is when similitudes occur. They are more prone to change or conform to like-minded people. If someone is commanding and a leader who is close to you, you are more likely to listen and do what they suggest.

How did TV sitcoms use canned laugh tracks for years? If marketers managed to generate audience laughter and higher ratings, they wouldn't use these. Part of the reason you laugh along anyway, and despite yourself, is how you determine what action is socially "right." If you're not sure how to act, then you rely on those around you (or in the audience on virtual television) to help you find a way to react appropriately. If others do that, then that must be the right thing to do. This law works to encourage new prospects to buy your services or products if you rely on testimonials from satisfied customers or customers (unscripted ones are the best). The law can also be used to convince your sponsor, client, or team that others are following suggestions similar to yours. People want to feel as though they are parts of an established community that already knows where they are going.

Using the Laws of Persuasion

Good negotiations generate win-win or mutually beneficial outcomes; that is, outcomes that all parties believe they have received a good deal. A good deal isn't always the same for all; negotiators often use different criteria to judge the success of their negotiating results. Finding "hard" negotiators using manipulative tactics based on the Laws of Persuasion isn't unusual. You should call attention to these strategies and steer the conversation towards a more realistic solution. You can also try to avoid law-based coercion by setting ground rules or preconditions in advance that will prohibit these tactics by using only rational standards as a normal negotiating process.

Ethical Issues

Though these laws in and of themselves are neither good nor bad, they can easily be used for positive or negative results. The regulations should only be used in a setting that tries to obey ethical rules to make lives better. Manipulation happens when you only exploit or deceive others for your gain.

2.2 Secrets methods of Persuasion

1. Spend time with the person

Time is a powerful technique for persuasion. The more time we spend with others, the more we are in a position to influence them. Time promotes confidence. If parents want to influence their kids, they will stay with them for some time. If workers wish to their colleagues to influence them, they should spend time with them. If you want to like people you dislike, spend some time with them. They'll love you eventually — or at worst, they'll hate you less.

2. Be likable

People tend to be helping people that they like. It's as easy to get people to like you instantly as displaying an eyebrow flash, a head tilt, and a smile. Restaurant waiting staff tend to offer customers they want better service. People who handle complaints tend to be more responsive to the individuals they want. People are more likely to miss faults, make exceptions to the rule, and go out of their way to accommodate people they like.

3. Change their minds before they say no

No one can read the minds, but by observing a person's mouth, you can come close. The lip purse is a slight rounding or puckering of the lips. Pursed lips mean the person with whom you are talking has developed a thought that is contradictory to what is being said or done. You get an advantage to know what a person thinks. The trick is to change one's mind before he can articulate any opposition. Once a person expresses an opinion or a decision aloud, the psychological concept of continuity makes it more challenging to change one's mind. People tend to stick to what they say, but not to what they think. If you see pursed lips, you will know what someone is thinking, and you will be able to use persuasion to change the minds of that person before he says no.

4. Don't stop at "You're Welcome"

When thanked, most people respond, "You're welcome," but added, "I know you'd do the same for me," to make your response more powerful. This invokes the psychological principle of reciprocity. If people get something concrete or even something intangible like a compliment, they're predisposed mentally to give something in return. Reciprocity increases the chance of future requests being complied with.

4. Add a Sense of Wonder

The introduction of a sense of wonder in conversation or as self-talk also increases the likelihood of compliance. People typically want to talk about their expertise with others. This tendency leverages the introduction of a sense of wonder. If you need assistance with a job, seek out a person with that ability, and simply inquire throughout your conversation, "I'm working on this project, and I'm having some difficulty. I was curious if you might have run into the same problem." An expert in the field would find it difficult not to contribute his knowledge, just to demonstrate his mastery. He may even offer his services to help you resolve this issue. This creates the illusion that the specialist provides experience and is not being asked to provide free advice or services.

Persuasive individuals have an uncanny ability to make you lean towards their thought. Their likeability is their secret weapon. They get you to appreciate more than their ideas; they earn you like them.

Here are the 15 tricks of the trade used to their advantage by exceptionally persuasive people.

They Know Their Audience

Persuasive people know their audience inside and outside, and they use this information to speak the language of their audience. Whether it's toning down the assertiveness when talking to someone who's reserved or cranking it up for the violent, high-energy sort, everyone is different, and catching on to those subtleties goes a long way towards getting them to understand your point of view.

They Connect

People will accept much more what you have to say once they have a sense of what kind of person you are. Stanford students were asked to reach an agreement in class during a negotiation test. Fifty-five percent of the students successfully reached agreement without any kind of instruction. However, 90 percent of the students did so successfully when they were instructed to introduce themselves and share their backgrounds before trying to reach an agreement.

The goal here is to avoid getting too wrapped up in the debate back and forth. The person you are talking to is a person, not an adversary or a target. No matter how convincing your point, if you don't communicate on a personal level, he or she will doubt all you're saying.

They Aren't Pushy

Persuasive people assertively and confidently articulate their proposals, without being offensive or pushy. The pushy people are an enormous turn-off. The in-your-face method begins backpedaling the receiver, and they're running for the hills before long. Persuasive people don't ask for much, and they complain not vehemently for their position because they realize that subtlety is what wins people in the.

They Aren't Mousy

On the other hand, it seems flawed and unconvincing to present your ideas as questions, or as if they need approval. If you appear to be quiet, concentrate on posing your thoughts as statements and interesting facts to mull over with the other side. Take qualifiers off your speech as well. There's no room for "I think" or "it's possible that" when you're trying to be persuasive.

They Use Positive Body Language

Becoming aware of your gestures, expressions, and tone of voice (and making sure they're positive) will engage and open people to your arguments. Using an enthusiastic tone, uncrossing your arms, keeping eye contact and leaning towards the person speaking are all forms of positive body language used by persuasive people to draw others into. Positive body language will get your audience engaged and convince them that what you say is valid. When it comes to persuasion, it may matter more how you say something than what you say.

They Are Clear and Concise

Persuasive people can have their ideas communicated quickly and clearly. When you have a firm grasp of what you're talking about, it's fun and easy for those who don't understand to explain it. A good strategy here is to get to know your subject so well you can explain it to a kid. If you can adequately justify yourself to someone who has no experience on the subject, you can make a compelling argument with someone who does.

They Are Genuine

To be convincing, it is essential to be genuine and honest. Nobody wants a fake. People are gravitating towards actual people because they know they can trust them. It's hard to believe someone when you don't know who they are and how they feel.

Persuasive people know who those people are. We are relaxed enough in their skin to feel comfortable. By focusing on what drives you, and making you happy as an individual, you become a person that is much more interesting and persuasive than if you try to win over people by trying to be the person they want to be.

They Acknowledge Your Point of View

To concede, the point is an extremely potent tactic of persuasion. Admit your argument isn't perfect. This shows you are open-minded and willing to make adjustments, rather than sticking stubbornly to your cause. You want to know that your audience has their best interests at heart. Try to use statements like, "I see where you come from," and, "That makes a lot of sense."

They Ask Good Questions

The biggest mistake people make when it comes to listening is not hearing what is being said because they're focusing on what they're going to say next or how it's going to affect what the other person is saying. The words are loud and clear, but the meaning is lost. To avoid this, a straightforward way is to ask a lot of questions. People like to know that you are listening, and something as simple as a question of clarification shows not only that you are looking but also that you care about what they say. You'll be surprised just by asking questions about how much respect and appreciation you gain.

They Paint a Picture

People are much more likely to be convinced by something with visuals that bring it to life. Persuasive people make use of powerful visual imaging to capitalize on that. These people tell vivid stories that breathe life into their ideas when the actual images aren't available or appropriate. Good stories create images that are easy to relate to and hard to forget in the recipient's mind.

They Leave a Strong First Impression

Most people decide if they want you or not within the first seven seconds of meeting you. Instead, they spend the rest of the conversation explaining their initial reaction internally. This may sound terrifying, but by knowing this, you can take advantage of it to make enormous gains in your likeability and persuasiveness. First impressions are closely connected to positive body language. Healthy posture, a firm handshake, a smile, and opening your shoulders to the person you're talking to help make sure you get an excellent first impression.

They Know When to Step Back

Urgency is a direct threat to conviction, so walk lightly. Studies show that when you try to force people to agree instantly; in fact, they are more likely to stand by their original opinion. Your impatience causes them to oppose your arguments to their advantage. If you're powerful, you shouldn't be afraid to withdraw and give it time to sink in. Good ideas are often hard to process immediately, and a little bit of time can go a long way.

They Greet People by Name

Your name is an essential part of your identity, and when people use it it it feels terrific. Persuasive people make sure they use the names of others whenever they see them. You shouldn't just use someone's name if you greet him or her. Research shows that when the person they're talking to refers to them by name, people feel validated.

If you're great with faces but have trouble with names, have fun with it and make it a brain exercise to remember people's names. Do not be afraid to ask his or her name a second time when you meet someone, if you forget it right after you hear it. If you remember the next time, you see the person you will need to keep the name handy.

They Are Pleasers

Persuasive people never win the fight just to lose the war. They know how and when to stand their ground, yet they are making constant sacrifices that will help their cause. They're just giving in, giving land, and doing things to make other people happy. Persuasive people do this because they know this will win over people in the long run. They know that winning is better than being "right."

They Smile

Naturally (and unconsciously) people mimic the body language of the person they speak with. If you want people to like you and believe in you, during a conversation, smile at them, and they will unconsciously return their favor and feel good as a result. Persuasive people smile a great deal because they are genuinely enthusiastic about their ideas. That has a deadly effect on everybody they meet.

Seven Qualities of Powerful Persuaders

If you are the one who is persuading, then you need the following skills, attributes, and features that make you trustworthy and reliable.

Belief

Successful persuaders believe in themselves and the things about which they talk. After all, if you don't believe in what you say, how do you expect anyone else to believe in it?

Enthusiasm

I have known people who believe totally in what they say but do not communicate with any excitement or passion whatsoever. British people especially struggle with this; however, if you want to persuade someone, you'd better find a way to be enthusiastic about it.

Knowledge

You need to know what you're talking about, so make sure you have all the information, facts, figures, and statistics you need to put your case into practice.

Empathy

Consider yourself in someone else's shoes. What do you think of them as necessary? Take careful consideration of why they should accept what you say. If somebody is scared of flying, then there is no point in telling them not to be stupid and not to behave like a baby. You need to think about how you might feel in these situations and what could convince you to change your mind; you need to overcome the fear with benefits that are important to the person.

Persistence

If you want to convince someone, don't give up on the first "no" or deny what you are doing. Persevere and endure-but do well!

Others will not automatically respond to your honesty in a negative way when they know that you believe what you say. There is a fine line from being persistent in being a nuisance. Look at the reactions of the other person and if it looks like you continue too much-stop

Energy

Put energy into all the interactions you have with others. Enthusiasm for energy fuels; people are persuading us with power. Lots of TV presenters use their energy to sell their ideas to us. Think of the celebrity chefs on television that persuade us to produce fabulous meals or other presenters that make us all excited to remodel our homes or gardens.

Consistency

Everything that you do or say is necessary, it all counts. If you want to be a good persuader, then you have to be consistent. If you're trying to convince someone to keep their promises, then you always have to save yours. If you say-" I'm going to call you back in ten minutes, "later in nine minutes, phone them back.

You need a lot of skills, qualities, and characteristics to be a potent persuader. Even with all of them in place, success is still not guaranteed. People are more likely to be convinced, however, by people they trust, they like and have a good relationship with.

Chapter 3: Dark Psychology, Persuasion and Mind Manipulation

After discussing the laws and secrets method of persuasion. This chapter will discuss dark psychology, persuasion and mind manipulation techniques.

3.1 What is dark psychology?

They say power is knowledge. Well, if the experience is power, then having human psychology knowledge is the equivalent of having superpowers. Psychology, the understanding of the human mind, and how it works, is a central topic for human existence. Psychology underpins everything from advertisement to banking, from crime to religion, and from love to hate. Someone who understands the principles of psychology holds the key to human influence, a critical few others possess.

Obtaining knowledge of psychology is often a difficult task. Like all the most advanced secrets of humankind, psychological experience is buried deep within the pages of dense journals and kept out of reach of the public at large. To order to distill this powerful knowledge into a useful form, someone would need to dig through countless books and journals, trying to separate the valuable from the useless.

There's dark psychology in the world at work. You may not like this fact but you are unable to change it. So you have a choice: either you are trying to remain ignorant of something powerful and risk becoming your next victim, or you are taking control of your situation and learning to protect yourself and those you love from people who would ruin you through their ruthless psychological use. Understanding the dark psychology is not just a measure of defence. Inside the world of dark psychology there are ideas and principles that can help you make progress in your personal and professional endeavors. No one is asking you to become a psychopath. Still, perhaps in your Dark Psychology, you could use a little more power to research the human condition as it relates to people's psychological existence to prey on other people motivated by criminal and deviant drives that lack meaning and general theories of instinctual drives and the theory of social sciences. All humanity has the potential to harm other human beings and living creatures while this urge is restrained or sublimated by many, some act upon these impulses.

Dark Psychology seeks to understand certain emotions, feelings, beliefs, and mechanisms of subjective thinking that contribute to aggressive actions that are antithetical to contemporary human behavioral understandings. Dark Psychology assumes that criminal, deviant, and abusive behaviors are purposive, and 99.99 percent of the time has some rational, goal-oriented motivation. It is the remaining parts.01 percent, Dark Psychology from Adlerian theory and Teleology. There is a region within the human psyche that Dark Psychology postulates, allowing some people to commit atrocious acts without purpose. In this theory, the Dark Singularity was coined.

Dark Psychology posits that all humanity has a reservoir of malevolent intent toward others ranging from minimally obtrusive and fleeting thoughts to pure psychopathic deviant behaviors without any cohesive rationality. The Dark Continuum is called this. Mitigating factors that serve as accelerators or attractants to reach the Dark Singularity, and where heinous actions of an individual fall upon the Dark Continuum, is what Dark Psychology calls Dark Factor. Below is a brief introduction to those definitions. Dark Psychology is a topic that this writer has been struggling with for 15 years. It was only recently that he finally conceptualized the meaning, philosophy, and psychology of this human condition aspect — day-to-day life.

Dark Psychology encompasses everything that makes us who we are related to our dark side. This common cancer is present in all cultures, all faiths, and all of humanity. From the moment we are born to the time of death, within us, there is a side lurking all that some have called evil, and others have defined as criminal, deviant, and pathological. Dark Psychology presents a third philosophical construct that takes a different view of these behaviors from religious dogmas and theories of contemporary social science.

"It is the individual who is not interested in his fellow men who has the most significant difficulties in life, and who offers others the most considerable injury. It is from such people that all human failures spring up.

Some people commit these same actions in Dark Psychology posits and do so for power, money, sex, revenge, or any other known purpose. Without a target, they commit those horrid acts. Simplified, its ends don't justify its means. There are people who, for the sake of doing so, abuse and injure others. The capacity lies within all of us. The field which this writer examines is the potential to damage others without intent, reason, or intention. Dark Psychology assumes that this dark potentiality is incredibly complex and even harder to define.

Dark Psychology believes that we all have the capacity for predator behaviors and that potential has access to our emotions, feelings, and beliefs. We all have this potential as you will read throughout this manuscript, but only a few of us act upon them. At one time or another, we all had thoughts and feelings about wanting to behave brutally. We have all had ideas that we want to severely hurt others without mercy. If you're honest with yourself, you'll have to agree that you've had thoughts and feel like you want to do heinous deeds.

Because of the fact, we consider ourselves to be a kind of benevolent species, one would like to believe that these thoughts and feelings would not exist. Unfortunately, all of us have these thoughts, and fortunately, never act upon them. Dark Psychology suggests that there are individuals who have the same ideas, emotions, and experiences but act upon them in a deliberate or impulsive manner. The apparent difference is that they act upon them, while others have merely fleeting thoughts and feelings to do so.

Dark Psychology argues that this style of predator is purposive and has some rational, purpose-oriented motivation. Religion, philosophy, psychology, and other dogmas have been convincing in their attempts to define Dark Psychology. It is true that most human behavior, linked to evil actions, is purposeful and purpose-oriented. Still, Dark Psychology suggests that there is an environment where persistent behavior and purpose-oriented motivation tend to become nebulous. There is a spectrum in the victimization of Dark Psychology, ranging from perceptions to total psychopathic deviance, with no apparent logic or intent. This continuum, Dark Continuum, helps the Dark Psychology philosophy to be conceptualized.

Dark Psychology addresses that part of the human psyche or universal human condition that allows predatory behavior and can even compel it. Some of the characteristics of this behavioral tendency are its lack of apparent rational motivation, its universality, and its lack of predictability in many instances. This universal human condition is assumed by Dark Psychology to be different or an extension of evolution. Let's look at some fundamental evolutionary tenets. Second, consider that we evolved from other animals and are the perfection of all animal life at present. Our frontal lobe allowed us to become the creature at the apex. Now let us presume that being alpha predators doesn't exempt us from our animal instincts and predatory nature.

"The greater the sense of inferiority felt, the stronger the desire to conquer, and the more aggressive the emotional agitation becomes." Assuming this is true if you adhere to evolution, then you think that all action relates to three primary instincts. The three main human drives are age, violence, and the instinctual desire to self-sustain. Evolution follows the survival tenets of the fittest species and its replication. We and all other forms of life act in such a way as to procreate and survive. Aggression happens to mark our territories, defend our land, and eventually win the right to procreate. It sounds rational, but in the purest sense, it no longer forms part of the human condition.

Our power of thought and perception has made us both species apex and brutality practice apex. If you've ever watched a documentary about nature, this writer will surely cringe and feel sorry for the antelope ripped to shreds by a lion pride. Although brutal and unfortunate, the violence purpose fits in with the evolutionary self-preservation model. The lions are killing for food, which is necessary for survival. At times, male animals fight for the rite of territory or the will to power to death. All of these violent and brutal events demonstrate evolution.

"Defiant people will always persecute others, yet they will always find themselves oppressed." When animals hunting, they always harass and kill the group's youngest, weakest, or female. Although this fact sounds psychopathic, it is because of their preferred victims that their own risk of injury or death is minimized. That way, all animal life acts and behaves. All of their brutal, violent, and bloody actions relate to evolutionary theory, natural selection, and survival and reproductive instinct. As you will learn after reading this manuscript, when it comes to the rest of life on our planet, there are no applications of Dark Psychology. We, human beings, are the ones that embody what Dark Psychology is trying to explore.

When we look at the human condition, theories of evolution, natural selection and animal instincts, and their theoretical tenets, seem to dissolve. We are the only creatures on the face of the earth to prey on one another for the species' survival without the reason of procreation. Human beings are the only species that prey unexplained desires upon others. Dark Psychology discusses the part of the human psyche or universal human condition that enables predatory behavior and can even compel it. Dark Psychology believes that there is something intrapsychic that drives and is anti-evolutionary to our response. We are the only species to kill each other for reasons other than life, food, land, or procreation.

Dark Psychology also assumes that this dark side is unpredictable. Unpredictable in understanding who is acting on these dangerous impulses, and even more unpredictable in the lengths, some will go completely negated with their sense of mercy. Some people attack, kill, torture, and assault without cause or purpose. Dark Psychology speaks of acting as a predator seeking human prey without clearly defined goals to these actions. We are incredibly dangerous to ourselves as human beings and to every other living creature. The reasons for this are many and attempts by Dark Psychology to address certain hazardous elements.

The more readers can visualize Dark Psychology, the more prepared they become to reduce their chances of human predators being victimized. It is necessary to have at least a minimum understanding of the Dark Psychology before continuing. When you continue to expand this build through future manuscripts, this writer will go into the essential concepts in depth.

Six tenets are then required to grasp Dark Psychology as follows fully:

- Dark Psychology is a part of the human condition as a whole. This model has had a historical influence. All cultures, communities, and the people who live in them maintain this facet of human nature. According to the most compassionate men, they have this world of evil, but never act upon it and have lower rates of violent feelings and thoughts.
- Dark Psychology is the study of the human condition, as it relates to the thoughts, feelings, and perceptions of peoples related to this innate potential to prey on others without clear definite reasons. Since all action is purposeful, goal-oriented, and conceptualized by modus operandi, Dark Psychology puts forth the notion that the

closer a person comes to the "black hole" of pure evil, the less likely he/she has a motivational purpose. While this writer assumes that natural darkness is never attained as it is infinite, Dark Psychology assumes some come close.

- In its latent form, Dark Psychology may be overlooked due to its potential for misinterpretation as aberrant psychopathy. History is full of examples of this latent propensity to manifest itself as aggressive, destructive behaviour. Current psychiatry and psychology describe the psychopath as an unrepentant abuser for his actions. There is a continuum of severity in Dark Psychology posits ranging from thoughts and feelings of violence to severe victimization and violence without reasonable purpose or motivation.

- In this continuum, the Dark Psychology's severity is not deemed less or more heinous by victimization behavior but plots out a range of inhumanity. Comparing Ted Bundy and Jeffrey Dahmer would be one easy example. Both psychopaths were severe, and their actions were heinous. The difference is that Dahmer committed his atrocious assassinations for his insane need for companionship when Ted Bundy was assassinated and sadistically caused suffering from pure psychopathic madness.

- Dark Psychology believes that every human being has a potential for violence. In all humans, this potential is innate and various internal and external factors increase the likelihood that this potential will manifest into volatile behaviors. These behaviors are inherently predatory, and can sometimes function without reason. Dark Psychology believes psychological interpretations of the predator-prey relationship. Dark Psychology is simply a human phenomenon and no other living creature experiences it. In other living organisms, aggression and mayhem can exist, but humanity is the only species capable of doing so without intent.

- An understanding of Dark Psychology's underlying causes and triggers would better allow society to recognize, diagnose, and possibly reduce the dangers inherent in its influence. Learning Dark Psychology principles has a valuable dual purpose. Second, by acknowledging that we all have a capacity for wrong, those with this information will reduce the likelihood that it will explode. Second, understanding Dark Psychology's tenets ties in with our original evolutionary purpose of struggling to survive.

If you've been a victim of the Dark Psychology guided predator, don't feel humiliated because at one time or another, we all experience some form of victimization in our lives. We have a dark side to all of us. It is part of the human condition, but it has agreed not to be understood well. Dark Psychology, an unpleasant reality, encircles us waiting patiently to pounce. As previously mentioned by this writer, Dark Psychology embraces all forms of cruel and violent behaviour. We only need to look at the senseless animal cruelty. Being a devoted pet lover, this writer's abuse of animals is both vicious and psychopathic. As recent studies have suggested, the mistreatment of animals correlates with a higher likelihood of committing violence against humanity.

On the Dark Continuum's milder side is the abuse of other properties or the rising levels of violence in video games children and teens begging for during the holiday season. Vandalism and the need for a child to play violent video games are mild compared to overt violence but are clear examples of this universal human characteristic demonstrated by this writer's theory. The vast majority of humanity rejects and conceals its existence, but in all of us, the features of Dark Psychology nevertheless lurk silently beneath the surface.

It's universal across society, and everywhere. Some religions describe it as a force which they call Satan. Some cultures believe that demons are the culprits that trigger malicious actions. Dark Psychology has been defined as a psychiatric condition by the brightest of many religions or spawned by genetic traits passed down from generation to generation.

Many of these crimes show themselves throughout history. The holocaust currently unfolding in neighboring countries after World War II and ethnic cleansing are just a few examples. History abounds with stories with the traces of what Dark Psychology has produced. Dark Psychology is alive and well, and a close inspection is required. A theoretical basis of comprehension will gradually grow as you continue to explore the theories and principles of Dark Psychology.

3.2 Mind Control Techniques

Here is a bird's eye view of some standard mind control techniques that can help you to improve your lives:

1. Visualization

We train our minds to work towards success by visualizing ourselves attaining success. Read some helpful visualization tips in our article. Positive energy can be attracted.

However, insurmountable the target may seem; we are attracting good luck through positive visualization! Sports psychologists make extensive use of this approach to achieve peak performance in athletes.

2. Meditation

Meditation is one of the oldest mind control methods. We allow peace and relaxation to flow through our minds by relaxing the mind and emptying it of all thoughts. Meditation quiets disparate thoughts constantly fluttering through our mind and gives its voice to our subconscious.

The alpha waves emitted by the mind, peak after meditation, are scientifically proven. Alpha waves enrich creative thinking and positive. Meditation allows the mind to focus on the moment, and only on what matters.

3. Mirror Talk

Man is his best friend and the worst enemy of all. Negative self-talk is becoming a prophecy which fulfills itself. Speaking to oneself can always be a surefire way for all to look down on.

On the other hand, if we give ourselves positive strokes and encourage ourselves, the mind feeds and focuses on what can be achieved, and works towards that goal.

4. Self-Hypnosis

Like meditation, self-hypnosis empties the spirit of all thoughts and focuses the mind on a single goal. Self-hypnosis and repetition of an only mantra is a technique that Alcoholics

Anonymous has used successfully to free alcoholics from their self-destructive dependence on alcohol.

5. Writing Down the Goals and Continuous Self-Assessment

Writing down our goals provides a concrete form for them. Continuously reviewing goals and making progress towards achieving them will enable you to make the changes necessary. It also helps to keep your purpose constant and spirits up-to-date.

3.3 Persuasion Tips for Everyday Use

If you are looking to influence people, merely understanding the principles underlying persuasion isn't enough. You also need to learn the simple yet effective ways you can use those concepts in everyday life.

If you're a persuasive person, you'll have a much easier time in life, and your intended results will often be achieved without having to jump through the hoops. Some of the tips to be more convincing can be quickly applied, while others will require a bit of practice.

Tip - 1

Appear assured Trust doesn't come naturally to us all. Many people seem to be relaxed more quickly while others are struggling quite a bit. Whether or not you are usually confident, you need to ensure that you always appear optimistic to others. If you're nervous about how you look at a particular topic or your skills, nobody else needs to know that. Do not provide a platform for your insecurities to shine on. Instead, fake it until you make it.

In this country, some people don't know a lot of things and yet have managed to get scores of people to help them and their ideas. Rationale? They reflect the epitome of confidence. They walk into the rooms, as if they were their own. We act authoritatively even when they're uncertain what they're talking about. Faith means you know what you're talking about. Things allow people who know what they're talking about to believe themselves.

Tip - 2

Be careful with your response. Even when you let yourself be convinced to do something, most people like to think it was their idea to do something first. No one wants to believe that they have allowed a particular concept to be shoved down their throats. You have to be discreet in your approach to a persuasion for performance. Consider starting with an anecdote rather than presenting a particular subject in full-on. If you are looking to get someone to buy into an investment, start by mentioning how you and your friends went on a cruise last weekend after receiving your Investment X payout. Don't even try to sell them that investment. Instead, get the other person to think about how they might have gone for the cruise too if they had invested in the investment vehicle. In short, entice people with your tentation without being too obvious.

Tip - 3

Be versatile with your techniques. Persuasion methods are not set in stone. Different people react to different stuff. The same person will also respond to different ways differently depending on time and occasion. You need to know when to switch gears as needed. Sometimes you will have to work with the liking principle, and some other times you will have to base your method on the authority principle. Reading social signals will allow you to decide what methods to use.

Tip - 4

Timing is all if you want to convince someone to buy a house, you'll be more effective if you catch them when they go shopping for homes. Some things hold that true. If you want your crush to go from crush to girlfriend, when you talk to them when they are looking for a relationship, you will have an easier time. You also have to master the art of knowing when the timing is right, to master the art of persuasion. If not, you'll fall into the trap of pressuring people to come to terms with things they're not interested in. No one likes a person who continually plagues them into doing something, particularly in the strangest times.

Tip - 5

Being an exciting bonus is not dull for most convincing people. No one pays a lot of attention to annoying people. To converse with boring people is not fun. They're not engaging, and definitely, they're not memorable. If you want to win convincingly, you have to be an exciting person. The good news is that there are lots of exciting places to be. You just have to recognize and highlight something special about yourself for the world to see. It might be a talent or a hobby you're very good at. Maybe it's also your sense of humor or the way you dress. Perhaps you'd even want to share your unique worldview with your audience. Whatever you're going for, make sure it helps people remember you well after the conversation is over.

Tip - 6

Listen more than you're talking you might think persuasive means are talking a lot, but that couldn't be any further from the truth. You have to train yourself to be a good listener to be influencing people. Skills in listening serve two purposes. First, as long as people speak and you listen, it ensures that you gain crucial information that you can use to your advantage. Second, guys like a good listener. Why? For what? Because people just love to talk about themselves. Keep your mouth shut and your ears open, and you'll be on the right track to increase your likelihood quotient. If you don't think this is important when it comes to influencing others, please refer to the same theory, as mentioned in the previous section.

3.4 How to create a Connection

It can be exciting and nerve-wracking to get to know someone for the first time. Whether it's someone you met on a dating app or someone your best friend set you up with, it can be tricky to figure out a new person—but it doesn't have to be that. There are many simple things you can do to help you build a secure connection with someone new, from telling them about your likes and dislikes to doing a fun activity together.

Creating a bond with someone new can be as simple as asking them various questions to get to know them better. "Ask your date about their family. Talking to your potential partner is great, but it can also make a difference where you speak to them. Here are seven things you can do to build a connection with someone new.

1. Go on an Adventure

Turning your data into a scheduled adventure such as horseback riding or hiking can help create shared experiences with someone new. And, it could be an unplanned experience that you can make the most of. "When you get a flat tire, miss your reservation for dinner and have to make your fun out of an unexpected situation." These are the ways you bond — through shared experiences, and even more so when the lessons lead to adventure.

2. Take Time to Have a Conversation:

Going to the movies is a classic move on a date, but it doesn't give you a lot of chances to get to know your friend. "If you're going to a movie, make sure you've got the same amount of time outside the theatre, whether it's over dinner, coffee, or long walk home together, so you can figure out if you're connected.

3. Ask Open Questions

Asking questions that can begin with "how" or "what" will help conversations flow. Asking someone what is their favorite book, or how they got into their career, can lead to exciting responses that will help you build a bond with this new person. "Another way is to say 'say me more' that allows the person the room to focus on what they're thinking about.

4. Try Being Non-Judgmental

The key to building a connection with a new partner is to be open-minded when you start a new relationship. "Choose to listen in an open and unjudged manner." We don't have to agree with the perspective of the other person, just be open to understanding it so we can better understand and appreciate them.

5. Do an Activity Together

While no adventure needs to be every first date, doing any activity with someone new is a great way to build a connection with them. "When you're doing an activity-based event, your brain is firing neurons during the social activity and soaking in the novelty of the experience. An enjoyable date is something that you and your new partner would be able to bond about as your relationship grows, and doing anything as easy as playing mini-golf or taking a museum tour will help build your connection.

6. Go To A Busy Place

It could be enticing to get some time alone with the new person you're seeing, but being away from other people could put too much pressure on you and your date. "Go to a busy place to talk about things and break the ice." Find a happening place and look at the people, and enjoy the atmosphere. That's a great way to feel comfortable.'

7. Be Positive

Feeling excited about the prospect of starting a new relationship will help build a bond with someone new. "Smile and be grateful for the opportunity for true love. Don't sweat the little things. They're as nervous as you are, so let go and be kind and leave critical energy at home." Dating can be frustrating, stressful, and exhausting, but try to get in with a positive attitude— you might be surprised at how much your perspective might change.

3.5 Create an Expectation

The Expectations Rule uses expectations to influence reality and produce results. Individuals tend to decide how others expect them to behave. As a consequence, people meet those expectations, whether positive or negative. Expectations have a powerful impact on those we trust and respect, but an even more significant effect on perfect strangers, interestingly. Once we know that somebody wants something from us, we'll try to satisfy him or her to gain respect and obligation.

You've probably heard the saying, "What's being measured gets done." The same applies to expectations. What is currently predicted is what happens. People are rising up to meet their expectations. This is a powerful force that can lead to a person being uttered or destroyed. You can express doubts, lack of TrustTrust, and skepticism, and you'll see the results. When you believe in someone, trust them, and expect them to succeed, you'll see different results. Those who believe in our capacity are doing more than stirring us up. We create an atmosphere for us, in which success is more comfortable. If you build perceptions, you change the behavior of people. The action is expected whenever you label specific behaviors or characteristics. You can see frustration, disappointment, surprise, or dissatisfaction when those expectations are not met.

We express our goals in a sophisticated manner. It may be through our language, the inflections of our voice, or our body language. Just think of a time when someone was introduced to you. Usually, if you present yourself by your first name, then you do the same. You do likewise if they give their first and last names. Whether you realize it or not, you accept other people's indications about their expectations and act accordingly. Likewise, we are all unknowingly sending out our signs and expectations. The power is consciously employing the Rule of Expectations!

Numerous studies have shown how the Law of Expectations significantly affects the success of the citizens. For one study, for example, girls who were told to perform poorly on a math test did not perform well. In other assembly line workers who had been exposed, their job was complex completed at the same task less efficiently than those who had been told it was simple. Another case study showed that adults who received complex labyrinths solved them more quickly when they were told they were difficulty based on a grade school level.

In incorporating the Law of Perceptions to your powerful arsenal, you can adjust the perceptions of your audience — and their expectations of purchasing your product, service, or concept — and you'll be even more compelling. Most of us learned about the famous experiments on the Pavlov dogs. Ivan Pavlov, a physiologist who won a Nobel Prize, taught dogs to sound like a buzzer to salivate. The training was successful because when they heard the bell — the law of standards — the dogs had learned to expect food. In a way, the dogs behaved because the Rule of Expectations was at work. Shockingly reminiscent of Pavlov's experiments, the Rule of Expectations has ever since been used in advertising to make people salivate when viewing a particular brand of food commercially or thinking about it.

Expect with Confidence: Often, our expectations are based on the assumptions we have regarding individuals or groups of people. The same applies to us. Have you ever realized how your life expectancies become a reality? The expectation is, literally, a prophecy which fulfills itself. That is what we do consciously and subconsciously. Remember the kid who was always really loud and disruptive in grade school? Sometimes if people already believe that they are viewed in some way, then that's just how they're going to act, even if they don't intend to. In grade school, the loud kid knew he was perceived as disruptive by everyone, and so he was. The teacher was expecting bad behavior and meeting expectations.

Expectations of Others Affect Behavior: Often, the expectations we create for others come true. When applied in the real world, that can have interesting effects. This section contains several examples of how expectations changed lives and persuaded other people's behavior. School teachers The teachers can be the greatest asset or the most significant negative influence in a child's life under the umbrella of expectations. We know what happens when a teacher marks a student as a "troublemaker," as it sets specific standards for the behavior of the student. We've seen the "slow learner," "stupid," and "ADD" labels become projections for future academic success for a student. There's the replacement teacher's tale that came to class and found a note from the regular teacher marking one of her students as a troublemaker and another as helpful. The substitute teacher started the course, searching for these two students. She treated them differently when he noticed them. When the teacher returned, however, she was amazed when she discovered that the replacement felt that the troublemaker was helpful, and the helper was trouble. She had mixed them up! The conduct of the children was based upon perceptions of the replacement. That is often referred to as collective marking. People tend to live up to their bestowed positive or negative label.

Grubby Day: Most schools have "dress-up days," where students every dress up for Halloween, Spirit Day, Pajama Day, or Fifty Day, for example. They had a "Grubby Day" in one high school. As you can imagine, the student behavior on that particular day was less than outstanding. On this day, the administration received more complaints about the behavior of the students than any other. Some standards were set up by the dress code, which further set some expectations. Then, of course, the bad behavior met the expectations.

Littering: We know the kids tend to place their trash directly on the floor. At one elementary school, individually wrapped pieces of candy were given to students. Most wrappers, of course, ended up on the floor, and not in the garbage can. The teacher frequently commented on how neat and tidy the kids were during the next two weeks. On a classroom visit, the principal remarked to the kids that their classroom was one of the school's neatest and cleanest. Even the custodian had written a note on the blackboard telling the kids how pure and clean their class was. The children were given individually wrapped pieces of candy once again at the end of the two weeks. The majority of the wrappers ended up in the trash can this time.

Parental Expectation

One thing you notice about kids and toddlers is that they are acting according to their parents' standards. When I was young, I found that children would look at their parents while they fell down or bruised their heads when running and playing, so that they would know how to react. If the parents showed great concern and pain in their eyes, the kids would start crying in an effort

Blood Drive

When blood drive organizers make reminder calls, they may end their conversations with something like, "Then we'll see you at 10:00 a.m. tomorrow, okay?" and then wait for the commitment of the person. And why are they doing this? Research has shown that attendance rates increase dramatically as you build anticipation.

Sales Applications

When you engage the emotions in your tactics, the power of suggestion can be beneficial too. For instance, when your car salesman says, "You will love how this car handles the mountains," he shifts the focus away from the sale and creates a new image in your head. He also speaks as if you had already agreed to the sale because you wouldn't drive it in the mountains unless you buy it. He's acting like a done deal — and the truth is, the more he's doing this, the more! I love to see salespeople door-to-door use this law to their advantage. They approach a door, ring the bell, and tell the prospect with a big smile that they have an excellent presentation that the person needs to see. They use this strategy, of course, while wiping their feet on the doormat of the person in anticipation of being let in the house. You'd be surprised to see how often this technique does work. In expectation of signing the contract, you know the salesperson handling the prospect of his pen. Have you ever felt bad leaving a store or situation in which you didn't buy anything? The store has created the expectation you'd be making a purchase.

3.6 Steer the Person to your Point of View

There are ten basic ways to steer the person to Your Point of View.

1. Prepare

Before you speak, you have to think: what will appeal to other people? Who's that? What are its hot buttons? What is the most you can achieve in this conversation, realistically? How are you going to react when they say X? And so forth.

2. Connect

Find some bond between you and the other person. People are persuaded by people that seem like them. Find some commonality to build on (e.g., background, interests, culture).

3. Listen

Be quiet. Really, listen to exactly what the other person is saying. Pivot (change pitch) as required. Watch the body language.

4. The Law of Scarcity

People want what they can't have. Think about ways to make your proposal time-sensitive, exclusive or rare. Someone might just jump to your offer before it's too late.

5. The Rule of Consistency

Get small concessions or recognitions you can turn into bigger ones. People like to think coherently about themselves. Metaphorically speaking, get your foot in the door and then press for more.

6. Mental Shortcuts

People aren't fond of lengthy analysis. Give somebody an easy way to get to the conclusion they want. For example, individual retailers would increase the price of a product so long as it is not easily comparable with other items for sale-because consumers feel that something expensively priced has to be of high quality. Many people simply take a shortcut in their thought, instead of a full analysis.

7. Herding

When you demonstrate that others are already doing it, you will increase the chances of' making a sale'-and produce good results. We're just herders.

8. The Rule of Reciprocity

Bring a sense of duty. Do something for another and in return he/she wants to do something for you.

9. Be Patient

If you're trying to rush things up, you might be off-putting. Mirror the tempo of that other person. Don't try to get too much done too soon. Marketers suggest it takes seven "touches" to persuade someone to purchase.

10. Emotion

Locate an emotion in your listener to touch. Man buys with his heart and justifies with his brain.

Chapter 4: Dealing Against Persuasion

4.1 How to deal against persuasion

Here are the top 9 ways that the dealing against persuasion and how to both break them down or sustain them.

1. Inoculation

Medical inoculations work by giving you a little bit of the disease so your body will be able to get used to it and fend off a complete future attack. The same works for psychological inoculations against persuasion.

If people are already armed with counter-arguments, they find it easier to fend off attempts at persuasion.

- While persuading people: what counter-argument do they already know? In your attempt at convincing, avoid the' ordinary' claims. Use a new angle they haven't previously thought about.
- Resisting persuasion: expose yourself to various kinds of arguments and counter-arguments that you will likely face. When you know what's coming, it's easier to defend yourself psychologically. Look for indirect attempts at persuasion: maybe it's the same old argument made in a somewhat different way.

2. Forewarned is forearmed

It is much easier to marshal our defenses when we can see the attempt at persuasion coming. Blatant advertising, political party broadcasts, and the rest: our barriers are up, so it's more challenging to get through.

- Do not signal your attempt in advance while persuading: Try to divert attention from the attempt at persuasion by hiding it within a seemingly innocuous letter. Emphasize how you' just chat' or' think' about something.
- When resisting persuasion: try to spot attempts of persuasion enveloped in social pressure or as entertainment. For instance: "A bit won't hurt. Come on, this we all do! "Or:" Find out more about the secret love child. Insert TV network here "tonight.

3. Reactance

People don't like being told what to do or limited their rights. It can even result in a' boomerang effect' where people are telling people not to do something that makes them want to do something more.

- If persuading: avoid limiting the freedom of people, then make them feel that they have choices and space for maneuver and that can work to your benefit (see: affirm the right of choice).
- When resisting persuasion: consider whether the attempt to persuade you is restricting your freedom. If it is, then you should go with it? Alternatively, is the person accentuating how free you are to convince you?

4. Reality Check

People often perform a kind of reality check after being persuaded. Would I agree that I didn't mean anything? If I knew what I now know then, would I have decided? If not, then you cancel the entire thing!

- Do not give people time for a reality check while persuading them: Under the pressure of time, people find it hard to think.
- If you refuse persuasion: take a time-out afterward to decide whether you would still consent. Beware of time pressure or limited deals— these are designed to shorten rational processes and get us to jump right in.

5. Counter-arguing and bolstering

It's the most common defense of all: questioning why they're wrong (counter-arguing), and you're right (bolstering).

- To convince: firmly held convictions are hard to attack. Attempt to be sly to sidestep them. Minimize your point to make it less threatening or make the relationship appear more collaborative ("Hey, I'm just trying to work out the truth as much as you're a buddy")
- Resisting persuasion: think about who else is in agreement with you. By using social confirmation, this bolsters your position. Be careful about camouflaged attempts at persuasion.

6. Resistance Breeds more Resistance

If people defend themselves successfully against a convincing effort, their original location is stronger. Say I try to talk to you about dying your hair blue, and you think you're going to look ridiculous. Unless I put forward a better case than "because it's going to be funny," afterward, you'll be even more against it.

- If you convince: make your first attempt to persuade a good one, don't go half-hearted, or you might just increase long-run resistance.
- If you resist persuasion: if you know that the effort of persuasion is coming and you have counter-arguments ready, then your strength will only make you stronger.

7. Attack Authority

Persuasion attempts often use authority's argument, such as: "I am your father, so I know best." But like any child, we want to rebel, so we attack authority.

- Make sure your credentials are rock-solid while persuading you. If they aren't, consider someone who has unquestioned authority. Naturally, people listen to those who have (or seem to have) power.
- Resisting persuasion: strike the message source. Use and assign negative emotions such as anger or frustration to the so-called figure of authority. Be extremely suspicious of anyone who relies purely on influencing power.

8. being sharp and alert

Once we feel healthy and ready, resistance is most comfortable. That's when you're better able to raise counter-arguments, maintain your position, spot attempts at persuasion coming in, and so on.

- Convincing: when people are tired, their defenses are down. Can they be worn down or their resistance blunted by a frontal assault if they are alert now? And, can you diminish their resistance motivation?

- When resisting persuasion: guard against fatigue. If you're starving, never go shopping, buy a car when you're desperate, or talk to a salesman when you're half-distracted. Recognize periods when you are going to be tired and close yourself to replenishing the energy levels.

9. Not listening

Sometimes the easiest ways of resisting persuasion are the simplest. You walk away, switch off the television, or screen the drone from other people by humming the theme into The A-Team.

- Do you have their full attention when persuading: If not, then performance is hard to be? Start with the most exciting part of the argument to draw them in once they're focused on you.

4.2 Unmasking Dark Persuader

Some of the main reasons people can resist persuasion include a feeling of being under pressure or a lack of trust or relationship with the person who is trying to persuade them. The Long Con can overcome those two problems. The Long Con involves the dark persuader taking their time to earn the confidence of their victims.

They will be especially lovely to their victim to make sure they like the victim and trust them. This is usually achieved by creating unhealthy, artificial relationships, and other forms of rising levels of comfort.

Once the victim is mentally comfortable enough, the persuader starts their attempts. These usually begin with a particular insincere positive persuasion.

The persuader will lead their victim to make choices or perform some actions that are, in fact, for their benefit. That has a dual purpose.

Next, they get the victim used to being convinced by their persuader. Second, the individual creates a conceptual connection between persuasion and a positive result. So how does The Long Con perform? Let's take a victim as an example; a lady recently widowed, vulnerable by age and bereavement.

After her loss, she is friends with a man, maybe a relative, perhaps a member of her church. This guy then conducts small acts of constructive reinforcement, such as convincing her to have a better bank account or a way to cut her monthly bills. The victim appreciates these efforts and has confidence in his advice. The man then darkly persuades her to let him put some of her money into an investment. She obliges confidently. Naturally, the man takes everything from her that he can. If he's qualified, she'll end up feeling like he's genuinely trying to help her, and she's just got bad luck. Such is the profundity of dark persuasion. Graduality seems impossible when people hear about acts of dark coercion, such as people being spoken into suicide or murder. Who would do this sort of thing? People fail to realize that dark persuasion from nowhere is not always a big, sudden request. Alternatively, dark persuasion should be seen as a stepping stone. The persuader will cause one step at a time for the victim. That doesn't sound like a big deal.

They are a long way down before they know it, and the persuader will not let them back up. So how in the real-life would Graduality look like? Take the example of a psychopathic criminal who wanted to make others commit crimes on their behalf. If you can't imagine a person like this, think about gang bosses, cult leaders, or Charles Manson. This psychopathic criminal wouldn't start by asking someone to murder. They may begin by performing a small crime or by hiding a weapon for their persuader. No big deal. No big deal. Nevertheless, over time, the actions that the manipulator persuades his victim to perform are becoming ever more severe.

The persuader also has the unseen leverage of being able to hold the minor wrongdoings against the victim. The victim has a sense of being in too deep until they know it. They can easily be persuaded to commit even the most shocking crimes, for they have no other choice in their minds. Dark persuaders are experts at using Graduality to increase their persuasion's severity over time. They know their victims never jump over a canyon. So instead, the persuaders are building a bridge for them, little by little. Masking True Intentions There are various ways in which persuaders can use dark psychological principles to obtain what they want. Disguising the manipulator's true desires is a significant step toward an excellent dark persuasion. Depending on their target and situation, the strongest persuaders can use that strategy in different ways. One obscure psychological principle that the best persuaders use is the knowledge that it is difficult for many people to reject two requests in a row.

The victim may feel some form of compassion or guilt towards the persuader and may want to help them. The victim feels too awkward and can't refuse this second petition. Another way of masking true intentions during persuasion is reverse psychology, of a type. That means they'll refuse to go in the direction they're thrown, and veer off in the opposite direction instead.

If a dark persuader knows someone is a type of boomerang, then a fundamental weakness has been identified. Let's take a persuader whose friend tries to win over a certain girl, for example.

The persuader knows that this girl will be used and hurt by the mate. The girl is torn between a malevolent friend and an innocent third. The persuader will deftly steer the girl in the direction of the guy who is going to be good for her, knowing she is going to go against this and pick the harmful friend. Leading Questions As anyone who has ever met, a skilled salesperson will know when deployed in a careful and calibrated manner. Verbal persuasion can be very impactful.

One of the most effective tactics in a dark persuader's linguistic arsenal is the use of leading questions. These are questions that are meant to trigger a specific response in their victim. Every dark persuader with a little experience is well aware of the fact that they will resist and become less easily convinced if the victim starts to get the impression they are being led. If the persuader begins to feel that the victim is aware of what is happening, they will immediately switch tactics and only return to the leading questions after the victim has calmed down and regained their influential state. The State Transference State Law is a concept that refers to a person's general mood.

If someone is aligned in their thoughts, words, and deeds, then this is a powerful, congruent state example. State transference law involves the concept of the person holding the balance of power in any given situation, being able to transfer their emotional state to the person with whom they interact. When used by a dark persuader, this is a powerful concept.

4.3 Tips to Deal against Persuasion

- The only way to get an argument to its best is to avoid it.
- Show respect for the opinions of others. ...
- If you're wrong, then quickly and emphatically admit it.
- Start friendly.
- Gets the other person promptly, saying, "yes, yes."

4.5 How Manipulative Behavior Develops?

According to Stine's, manipulative behavior comprises three factors: fear, obligation, and guilt. "When someone manipulates you, you're psychologically coerced to do something that you probably don't want to do," she says.

Manipulative people mastered the art of trickery. They may seem decent and genuine, but often it's just a façade; it's a way of drawing you in and snatching you into a relationship before they show their true colors. Manipulative people are not interested in you except as a vehicle that allows them to gain control of their plans so that you become an unwilling participant. As many of you will acknowledge, they have several ways to do this. They often take what you say and do and twist it around so that what you have said and done will hardly become recognizable to you. They'll try to confuse you, and perhaps even make you feel like you're crazy. They distort the truth, and if it serves their end, they may resort to lying. The victim can be played by manipulative people, making you appear to be the one who caused a problem they began but who will not take responsibility for. They can be passive-aggressive or nice for one minute and standoff the next, keeping you guessing and prey on your fears and insecurities. Often they do make you defensive. Often, they can be extremely aggressive and abusive, resorting to personal attacks and ridicule, relentless in their search to get what they want. They are bullying and threatening and will not let go until they wear you down.

Nine characteristics of manipulative people imitate, so when one comes your way, you'll know what to look out for. Learning these underlying mechanisms of action will help prevent you from getting pulled into a deceptive connection. Staying alert, staying in touch with what you know is real about yourself, and anticipating what is to come will allow you to avoid conflict and maintain your integrity.

1. Manipulative people either lack insight into how they engage others or create specific scenarios, or they genuinely believe that their way of dealing with a situation is the only way because it means their needs are being met, and that's all that matters. Ultimately, all conditions and relationships are about them, and it doesn't matter what others think, feel, and want: "Controllers, abusers, and manipulative people aren't questioning themselves. They aren't asking themselves whether they are the problem. They always say somebody else is the problem.
2. Manipulative people do not understand borders. They are relentless in pursuing what they want and have little consideration as to who gets hurt along the way. They're not concerned about crowding into your space— physically, emotionally, psychologically, or spiritually. We lack

understanding or just don't know about what personal space and identity mean. They can be compared to a parasite-this is often an acceptable relationship in the natural world. However, in human behavior, feeding off someone is depleting, exhausting, weakening, and demeaning at their expense.

3. A manipulator shuns responsibility for his behavior by blaming others for causing it. It is not that it is the responsibility of manipulative people who do not understand. They do; a dishonest person simply sees nothing wrong in refusing to take responsibility for their actions, even when they make you take responsibility for yours. They will eventually try to get you to take responsibility for satisfying their needs, leaving no room to fulfill yours.

4. Manipulative people are prey to our sensibilities, emotional sensitivity, and, in particular, conscience. You know they're going to have an excellent chance to draw you into a relationship because you're loving, sensitive, caring, and of course, you want to help. At first, they will care for your goodness and kindness, always thanking you for the beautiful person that you are. But over time, appreciation for these values will be diluted because you are being used to represent someone who doesn't care for you. They just really care what you can do for them.

5. If you want an easy way of discerning manipulators from empathic people, pay attention to how they relate to you about others. Sometimes, they talk about you behind your back the same way they talk about others to you. They are masters of "triangulation" — creating scenarios and dynamics that allow intrigue, rivalry, and jealousy, and encouraging and fostering disharmony.

6. Never waste your time trying to explain to people committed to misunderstanding you who you are. If anybody doesn't get you, don't wait until they do stick around. Don't make them understand your mission, and like you — they don't care about you as a human being.

7. Characterize people by their acts, and their words cannot deceive you. Note also that what a person is saying and doing is two very distinct things. Watch someone closely without giving them excuses— usually, what you see is what you get.

8. If the individual makes as much effort to become the right person as they do to claim to be one, they may be the right person. This is an essential point: Our initial encounter and perception of someone strongly color our relationship with them in development. Unless we knew from the start that a person is not who they seem to be and just hides behind a façade what appears to be socially acceptable behavior, then we might be more cautious about getting involved.

9. Check frequently over what you think. That we're not doing enough. Our beliefs and attitudes change as life progresses, and we need to know how these changeable ideas influence us. When we're not sure what we believe, it's all too easy to allow someone else who's convinced their convictions are right— not just for them, but for you as well— to try to manipulate your thinking: s "When it comes to controlling others, there's no better tool than lies. Because you see, people live by creeds. And it can manipulate beliefs. The only thing that counts is the power to manipulate the opinions.

4.6 The difference between persuasion and manipulation.

1. The purpose behind the attempt to convince another person,
2. The truthfulness and honesty of the method, and
3. The net benefit or effect on that person Manipulation implies persuasion to fool, manipulate, or to induce the person on the other side of the discussion to do something, to believe something or to buy something that leaves them harmed or unprofitable. It can also mean you mask a desire to move them to your point of view in a way that will help you. And if this advantage were discovered, the discovery would make the other person far less open to your message because either it would: Demonstrate a strong bias against their lack of trade gain, demonstrate an ulterior motive for trying to persuade, often motivated by one-sided benefit, or some combination of both. So let's say, for example, I was selling a car to someone, and I had all my persuasion and strategic tools. That person walked into my dealership, and it was apparent they were looking for and genuinely needed a family-sized, affordable vehicle with a family of six children.

But then I took advantage of all my persuasive skills to persuade the father that he shouldn't buy a minivan, but rather a two-seater convertible to restore his youth, and in doing so, show his children how necessary it is to remain true to their youthful values, knowing full well that I would do the commission on that car twice and that it was inappropriate for them. That is tampering!

Now, what if that same parent with the same six kids came into my dealership and said to me, "Man, I just want to blow some cash. I would have to buy a six-seater. I know it's irrational, and I can't justify that, but I'm just jonesing about the two-seater convertible? "And what if I then used my persuasive abilities to lay out a conversation and a set of facts slowly and methodically that led this parent to understand the genuine benefit of buying a more affordable and suitable family car? That is persuasion rather than manipulation!

Because I used the same set of skills to convince someone to do something that I genuinely believed was in their best interest, rather than persuading them to do something that I was pretty sure was not in their best interest–and very likely with at least part of what I was talking about was less than truthful. Ultimately, persuasion strategies, tools, and an understanding of how to present facts, arguments, and interactions in a way that is more likely to get someone to buy into your point of view on the other side of the conversation are simply about persuasions.

It is the underlying intent, the net benefit, and the veracity with which you bring this toolbox to life that creates the difference between manipulation and persuasion.

4.7 Art of Persuasion in Business

You are a hard-working entrepreneur continuously looking for more customers and more money.

You may have tried to change the product plan many times, sell different services, or simply take on more customers to bring in more money.

But the art of persuasion, which is a science, was probably never taught at Business School. And I bet none ever told you how effective persuasion strategies could be for persuading more people to buy from you and more consumers to say yes to that plan or contract when used correctly.

So let's dig into a few essential techniques that you can begin to apply today:

The Art or Reciprocity

This is when someone does something or gives something to a person; then, it's normal for the individual to feel compelled to give back the favor. It's the same in business as well, and you have to start using this.

What can you give the customer free of charge to make the customer feel good but, at the same time, make them think they will provide you with something back or do something in return, such as working for you?

It could be as easy as a free one-page personalized report on the improvements that you can create for them. Or you could offer them one of your services or products, such as a website check-up or an eBook, DVD, or video for training.

It doesn't have to be expensive or cost you a lot, but it should be worth it. This approach builds confidence and enhances your relationship with your customers.

Start Small but be Consistent

This particular technique comes down to people acting inconsistent behavior. So once your customer makes a choice, they tend to behave in ways that are consistent with their decision.

What this means is that if you can initially get a potential customer to participate in a small action, such as purchasing your product or signing up for a lower-priced service, they are likely to accept more significant ideas or activities that you may throw at them after they are committed.

For example, let's say you got them to take up your basic SEO monthly service, so when you approach the next, you'll be more successful in securing them for a longer-term service or higher-priced product.

That's because once they've got their feet wet with you and when you've pleased them with their first purchase, they now have adequate information and some experience in dealing with you and what you're offering from which to make a judgment on further investment.

There's a reason why companies are giving away free samples, particularly for consumer products. Once you've had the chance to try it out, you're likely to make a point of consciously looking for it next time you shop and buy it. The same goes for you and that customer who comes back to try you out further.

Social Proof

If you've ever bought a product you didn't know about before landing on their Facebook page, ask yourself what made you buy it? You could cite price or what was included in the offer, but I guarantee that what pushed you over the edge and convinced you to buy was the gushing testimonials from people who filled the page below the buy button now. Many people tend to do or buy what everyone else is, particularly if they don't have previous experience of making their own decisions. That's why social evidence is one of the most popular and used methods in sales in the form of testimonials, whether written or video or comments. Showing pictures of customers and their rave reviews about the work you've done for them and the results you've given them on your website, forum, LinkedIn profile, and anywhere else that's important, is a sure-fire way to get more customers to work with you. The more influential or well-known the person or company is, the more potent that technique is to bring you into new customers. These people act as amazing endorsements for you, essentially saying to your potential customer, "If it's good enough for me, then it's good enough for you to work with it and so."

Celebrity Status

To command a lot of attention, gain more confidence, and have more authority, you don't have to be a celebrity, but it helps! So, by becoming the go-to person in your market, you can achieve that status. When you build up your experience and work with bigger and better clients, use this to cultivate partnerships with companies and consumers that you want to partner with by playing into your niche or market leader role. It comes with time, but you can help with the title you're using, highlighting your professional credentials if you've got them and any qualifications or specialized training you've received, in addition to the glowing testimonials. Of course, more people will step up to want to work with you.

The Likeability Factor

If the above technique now seems a little out of your reach, what about the good old test of likeability? It has been proved that customers are more likely to engage with the people they like in the business. If you are beautiful, of course, it helps. Yes, it's a proven fact that this plays an advantage in persuading others to work with you or doing something they wouldn't normally do–like taking you on that 6-month retention contract. Yet people like to engage with people who have the same interests as them, have been on the road similar to them, and have done well for themselves, or have identical pasts in which they may connect. In brief, people like them. More importantly, people buy from people they like and trust (which is why social media is so powerful) as you can show your online follower, community, and likeability, which then persuades others to work with you. Being proactive, fun, humorous, and passionate are also great ways to work with and do business with, too naturally.

Less is More

Most people want things they can't have, and if you make them scarcer or elusive, this applies to your products and services. I'm not talking about making it hard to work with or buy from you, but having a limited number of available packages or deadlines by which people can work with you, and a limited number of available spots. This encourages consumers to act quickly so that they don't miss anything unusual that works for you.

Putting your Techniques to Work

When you work through each of these strategies and adapt them to your existing way of working, you can certainly see a difference in your customer interactions and changes. You can attract new clients and referrals as a result of using the art of persuasion from the current customers you will enjoy continuing working with you.

Monitor the Negative Voice

Begin by monitoring your voice, which is harmful. Notice when you're self-critical, and watch the conversations going on in your mind. If you become aware of the conversations, then you can work to change them. Your job is to make sure the voice in your head is always positive and supportive and not negative and critical.

Friends & Family

Ask your family and friends about what your strengths are for their honest opinions. What do they think is right for you? When you were a kid, what were you good at? Write a checklist if you want an extensive review and ask them what they think about you in the listed areas. Ask a few people, and then you can see if the opinions are similar— just make sure that the person you're asking isn't jealous of you or would have reason to hurt you or offend you.

No Comparisons

Do not compare yourself to others — it's a disaster recipe. You just need to be good enough for yourself, so it doesn't matter what you have achieved with your sister, brother, friend, or enemy. Make your standards and set your personal goals.

Journaling

Look at yourself for a long time, and write a concise article. Journaling can be a great way to take an objective look at yourself. Tell your story how someone else's owns it. To what honestly do you think you're good at? Nobody needs to see what you're writing, just write to you. Write down all of your past accomplishments— start with last year and write about anything that went well, and then continue the list year after year, ensuring you include all of your accomplishments.

Personality Assessment

Do a Personality assessment, like the Myers Briggs or DISK personality profile quizzes. These assessments are a great way to understand yourself and to see how you fit in in the world; your strengths will become more apparent when you are familiar with your personality.

Create a Positive Environment

Make sure you are surrounded by people who love you and who support you. If criticism comes from outside sources, remove yourself from those environments that promote negativity. If you have no friends or members of your family who inspire and uplift you, join a community that will. There are many groups formed, both online and offline, to encourage people to live a happier and more positive life; join one.

Drown Yourself in Positivity

Create uplifting affirmations. Postpositive messages all over your home and work, and replace it with positive thoughts or words whenever you say something negative to yourself. The most important thing you need to remember is to be in control of your emotions. Some negative habits of the past can be broken, but you have to fill the void with constructive thoughts and words of encouragement.

Conclusion

Persuasion a mechanism by which the attitudes or actions of an individual are affected, without coercion, by communications from others. Certain variables (for example, verbal threats, physical intimidation, and one's physiological states) also influence one's attitudes and behavior. Not all communication is supposed to be persuasive; other aims are to educate or entertain. Persuasion also includes manipulating people, and many consider the exercise distasteful for this purpose. Others might suggest that the human community is disordered without some degree of social interaction and reciprocal agreement, like that achieved by persuasion. In that way, by considering the alternatives, the reasoning makes moral acceptability. During the Middle Ages, at the Universities of Europe, persuasion (rhetoric) was among the fundamental liberal arts that any educated man mastered; from the days of imperial Rome through the Reformation, preachers who used the spoken word to encourage any number of actions, such as virtuous conduct or religious pilgrimages, raised it to a fine art. In the modern era, persuasion in the form of advertising is most evident. Preliminarily, the persuasion mechanism can be studied by separating contact (as the cause or stimulus) from the related changes in attitudes (as the effector response).

Research has contributed to the delineation of a sequence of successive steps an individual is being persuaded to undergo. The message is provided first; the person pays attention to it and understands its contents (including the fundamental conclusion to be recommended and probably also the facts given in support). To order to be convincing, the person must give in or agree with the point that is being urged and, unless only the most immediate impact is of concern, must hold this new position long enough to act upon it. The ultimate goal of the persuasion method is to fulfill the actions suggested by the new attitudinal status for individuals (or a group); for example, a person enlists in the army or becomes a Buddhist monk or begins to eat a specific type of cereal for breakfast.

Some scholars stress parallels between education and persuasion, but not by any means everything. We hold that persuasion through clear communication closely resembles the teaching of new information. Therefore, because repetition in communication changes learning, they conclude that it also has a persuasive effect and that concepts of verbal learning and conditioning are commonly and profitably implemented by persuaders (such as in the moderate repetition of television advertisements, for example). The learning strategy seeks to accentuate message focus, comprehension, and retention.

One's reaction to persuasive communication is partly dependent on the message, and to a considerable extent on how it is viewed or interpreted. Words in a newspaper advertisement can exhibit various persuasive qualities if printed in red rather than black. Perceptual theorists find persuasion to alter the perception of any object of its attitudes by the individual. Perceptual methods often rely on evidence that the preconceptions of the recipient are at least as necessary as the content of the message when deciding what is to be understood. The approach stresses mindfulness and awareness. Although learning and perceptual theorists may stress the objective intellectual steps involved in the persuasion process, functional theorists emphasize more subjective aspects of motivation. Human beings are fundamentally ego-defensive according to this view— that is, social activities and beliefs work to fulfill conscious and unconscious personal needs that may have little to do with the objects to which those attitudes and behavior are guided. For example, the functional approach may theorize that ethnic discrimination and other forms of social hatred are derived more from the structure of individual personality than from knowledge about the existence of the social groups. Some theories consider the person faced with persuasive communication to be in the vexing position of seeking some reasonable compromise among many competing forces— e.g., individual preferences, established attitudes, new information, and social pressures from outside sources. Those who emphasize this model of conflict resolution (often called theoreticians of congruity, balance, continuity, or dissonance) focus on how people weigh these forces in changing their attitudes. Some thinkers who take this starting point emphasize the theoretical elements of persuasion, while others stress emotional factors. The extension of the model of conflict resolution is the model of persuasion for elaboration-likelihood (ELM), put forth by American psychologists. The ELM emphasizes the cognitive processing with which individuals respond to persuasive communications. According to this model, if people react by reflection on the content of the message and its supporting arguments too persuasive communication, the resulting change in attitude is likely to be more firmly established and more immune to counter persuasion. On the other hand, if people react with relatively little such reflection to persuasive communication, then the resulting change of attitude is likely to be ephemeral.

Each of the above methods appears to ignore one or more steps in the persuasion cycle and thus seeks to complement rather than supplant the others. A more diverse and holistic approach, based on the theory of information processing, is geared towards taking into account all the options suggested by the communication aspects of source, message, channel (or medium), recipient and destination (behavior to be influenced); each choice is evaluated for its persuasive effectiveness in terms of presentation, focus, interpretation, yield, retention,

Six fundamental principles of persuasion may automatically lead people to say "yes." Learning these concepts and related strategies will help you improve your control and, at the same time, protect against exploitation by others. In this review of "Manipulation: Persuasion Psychology," we will outline the six principles of persuasion briefly, how they function, and how they can be converted into tools of manipulation against us. The book discusses various psychological strategies that compliance professionals such as salespeople, waiters, car dealers, and fundraisers use to persuade us to say yes to something we would rather have said no to. Such techniques are six controlling weapons. Each of them forms the foundation for a chapter in the book.

References

- Exploring your mind. (n.d.). *Psychological Manipulation Techniques You May Be a Victim Of – Exploring your mind.* [online] Available at: https://exploringyourmind.com/psychological-manipulation-techniques-you-may-be-a-victim-of/.
- Regain.us. (n.d.). *6 Emotional Manipulation Techniques And How To Recognize And Stop Them | Regain.* [online] Available at: https://www.regain.us/advice/general/6-emotional-manipulation-techniques-and-how-to-recognize-and-stop-them/.
- Time. (n.d.). *How to Tell If Someone Is Manipulating You – And What to Do About It.* [online] Available at: https://time.com/5411624/how-to-tell-if-being-manipulated/.
- Psychology Today. (n.d.). *3 Reasons People Become Manipulative.* [online] Available at: https://www.psychologytoday.com/us/blog/communication-success/201912/3-reasons-people-become-manipulative.
- Psychology Today. (n.d.). *14 Signs of Psychological and Emotional Manipulation.* [online] Available at: https://www.psychologytoday.com/us/blog/communication-success/201510/14-signs-psychological-and-emotional-manipulation.
- Dr Jason Jones. (2020). *Dark Psychology & Manipulation: Are You Unknowingly Using Them?.* [online] Available at: http://drjasonjones.com/dark_psychology/.
- Lifehack. (n.d.). *4 Ways To Psychologically Manipulate Someone.* [online] Available at: https://www.lifehack.org/306016/4-ways-psychologically-manipulate-someone.

- Westmount Magazine. (n.d.). *Have you been a victim of manipulation at work? | Westmount Magazine.* [online] Available at: https://www.westmountmag.ca/have-you-been-manipulated-at-work/.
- decision-making-confidence.com. (n.d.). *Mind control explained - the dangers and how to protect yourself.* [online] Available at: https://www.decision-making-confidence.com/mind-control.html.
- GoodTherapy.org Therapy Blog. (n.d.). *Manipulation.* [online] Available at: https://www.goodtherapy.org/blog/psychpedia/manipulation.
- Superpower Wiki. (n.d.). *Mind Control.* [online] Available at: https://powerlisting.fandom.com/wiki/Mind_Control.
- Dr Jason Jones. (n.d.). *How to Avoid Being Manipulated - Dr Jason Jones.* [online] Available at: http://drjasonjones.com/how-to-avoid-being-manipulated/.
- Learning Mind. (n.d.). *8 Brainwashing Techniques Manipulators Use (without You Even Knowing).* [online] Available at: https://www.learning-mind.com/brainwashing-techniques/.
- Abuse Wiki. (n.d.). *Psychological manipulation.* [online] Available at: https://abuse.wikia.org/wiki/Psychological_manipulation.

- Lyons, M. (n.d.). The dark triad of personality: narcissism, Machiavellianism, and psychopathy in everyday life. Retrieved from

* https://www.amazon.com/Psychopathy-Everyday-Life-Anti social-Personality/dp/0275987981
* Lyons, M. (n.d.). The dark triad of personality: narcissism, Machiavellianism, and psychopathy in everyday life. Retrieved from https://www.amazon.com/Psychopathy-Everyday-Life-Anti social-Personality/dp/0275987981
* MD Anderson Cancer Center. (n.d.). Retrieved from https://www.mdanderson.org/
* Resource Lists. (n.d.). Retrieved from https://worc.rl.talis.com/lists/F86562C2-76C5-9F2C-2C4B-B1 9EEFD203A9/bibliography.html?style=oscola
* Sign Up for Newsletter Updates. (n.d.). Retrieved from https://press.princeton.edu/books/paperback/978069102584 1/the-psychiatric-persuasion
* U.S. Navy Memorial Site: Search Results. (n.d.). Retrieved from http://www.legacy.com/memorial-sites/navy/profile-search. aspx
* Peter Suedfeld. (n.d.). Retrieved from https://psych.ubc.ca/profile/peter-suedfeld/
* U.S. Navy Memorial Site: Search Results. (n.d.). Retrieved from http://www.legacy.com/memorial-sites/navy/profile-search. aspx
* Seiter, J. S., & Gass, R. H. (2004). Perspectives on persuasion, social influence, and compliance gaining. Retrieved from https://www.amazon.com/Persuasion-Social-Influence-Co mpliance-Gaining/dp/0815358210
* Persuasion. (n.d.). Retrieved from https://en.wikipedia.org/wiki/Persuasion

- Social Psychology Persuasion. (n.d.). Retrieved from **https://en.wikipedia.org/wiki/Social Psychology Persuasion**

- Influence : the psychology of persuasion. (n.d.). Retrieved from **https://www.worldcat.org/title/influence-the-psychology-of-persuasion/oclc/77527024**

- DellaVigna1, S., & Gentzkow21Department, M. (n.d.). Persuasion: Empirical Evidence. Retrieved from **https://www.annualreviews.org/doi/10.1146/annurev.economics.102308.124309**

- **Persuasion. (n.d.). Retrieved from https://en.wikipedia.org/wiki/Persuasion**